Evergreen

Winter 2004

Contents

Front Cover: "Sweet singing in the choir"... Choristers at Durham Cathedral hold lighted candles in front of a colourful arrangement of beautiful blooms. JOHN CROOK

Once on a Winter's Day

by Enid Pearson

The scene is all merry and bright as a white Christmas Day dawns at the Priory,

Hinton Charterhouse, near Bath, in Somerset.

Ramblers enjoying a healthy country trek through Downham, in Lancashire.

I'd like to go and see the old place again
Just once, on a winter's day,
Where frost makes white the lonely fields
And skies are silvery-grey

A robin waits patiently for spring in a bare tree on Dartmoor, in Devon.

Out where the beautiful fox runs free,
And the sunrise is gold in the sky,
Where woodlands are busy with squirrels and birds
In evergreen treetops high.

Ingleborough, in the Yorkshire Dales, looks like an iced cake on the landscape above Crina Bottom.

Mountain walking at the entrance to Coire Gabhail (the Hidden Valley) at Glen Coe in Argyllshire, Scotland.

I feel the old mysteries out on those roads,
Where our tread was deep in frost,
I recall the fireside, glowing with wood:
Those days will never be lost.

A branch of the River Wey is a gentle stream at Farnham, in Surrey.

For they live in my heart, though time has run,
And when something reminds me again
I think of your cottage out in the fields
And our winter walk down the lane.

Winter tranquillity beside the waters of Malham Tarn, in Yorkshire.

The Lord has blessed us with different lives
But we shall always be friends I pray,
And I'll never forget our walk down the lane
Once on a winter's day.

RURAL RIDES

The preserved steam railway known as the Mid-Hants Watercress Line runs for 10 miles between Alresford and Alton in Hampshire. Now one of the most popular attractions in the county, it provides a wonderful means of exploring these historic towns. The railway is run largely by volunteers and some paid staff, whose combined efforts have recreated a bygone age.

Before travelling on the Watercress Line, it is worth spending some time in Alresford. Originally known as Novum Forum, the town was later named New Alresford, meaning in old English "the ford over the river where the alder trees grow". The river is the Arle and alder trees still overhang it along an attractive river-

Steaming along the Watercress Line

side walk. Here only bird song can be heard. There is also the occasional "plop" as a brown trout takes an insect from the water's surface.

Several hundred years ago it was a more industrious scene. In 1189 Godfrey de Lucy became Bishop of Winchester and built the Great Weir in Alresford. This work dammed the River Arle and created Old Alresford pond, which was 200 acres in extent. Due to silting, it is now a more modest 30 acres and swans glide serenely on its surface. In its heyday the Great Weir provided the water power that drove several corn-grinding mills.

Further along the riverside walk is the Fulling Mill. Situated by a small weir, this attractive timbered and whitewashed building dates from the

Ramblers pass the Fulling Mill at Alresford in Hampshire, the town where the Watercress Line begins.

N.M. BROWNE

13th century. Once cloth was beaten and pressed there to make it into a closely woven, usable material. This was formerly done by human feet in a solution of fuller's earth, although water-driven hammers were later used.

At the end of the walk is Ladywell Lane, once the centre of the tanning industry in Alresford. Local names — such as Tanyard Barns — are a reminder of the days when animal hides were converted into leather. There is now a Millennium Trail in Alresford and a sign reads "The smell here some 200 years ago would have tested the best of stomachs".

Also nearby is Broad Street, with its lovely colour-washed Georgian buildings. These were erected after disastrous fires that broke out during the 17th century. Broad Street was once the home of the Alresford sheep fairs. The surrounding downland has always been most suitable for rearing sheep, with 140,000 animals present at the fair of 1837.

At the top of Broad Street is the church of St. John the Baptist. In the churchyard are the graves of four French Napoleonic prisoners of war, together with one of their wives. Among them is Pierre Garnier, formerly of the 66th regiment of

(continued)

infantry who died on 31st July, 1811.
Alresford was one of several towns in
Hampshire where French prisoners
were kept on parole. They signed a
pledge promising not to try to escape.
Forbidden to walk more than a mile
from the town during the day, the
prisoners were kept indoors at night.
Those who broke their parole were

held at the Swan hotel and removed
from the town. Many wild flowers
and trees can also be found in the
churchyard.

Not far from the churchyard is the
railway station, the headquarters of
the Mid-Hants Watercress Line. The
railway was opened in 1865, largely
due to the efforts of local business-
men and landowners. It brought
prosperity to Alresford because of the
highly prized crop of watercress. This
grew wild in the River Arle, a clear
chalkstream that still provides ideal
growing conditions. But with the
coming of the railway, watercress
was cultivated commercially for the
first time. It was taken by horse and
cart to Alresford station and then
transported to markets in London
and beyond.

The Mid-Hants finally closed in
1973. However, in 1977 a number of
steam railway enthusiasts decided to
re-open the line. Beginning at
Alresford, they relaid the track as far
as Ropley station and then Medstead
and Four Marks. In 1985 the 10-mile
length of track finally reached Alton.

Each of the four stations now
depicts a different era. Alresford station itself is a typical Southern
Railway station of the era 1923 to
1947. Milk churns are stacked on the
platform and gas lamps also add to
the atmosphere. Hanging baskets
adorn the station, too. The fuchsias in
these add a welcome touch of colour.
Then there are the advertisement
hoardings for such bygone delights as

Rain and Shine

All through the night
The cold rain falls,
On sleeping gardens,
Roofs and walls.
Disconsolate
The cat creeps in,
With drooping tail
Wet to the skin.
I dry him off
With fluffy towel
Despite his loud
Protesting yowl.
The rain it carries
On all day —
Will it never go away?
Then suddenly
The sun's about,
The rain dries up,
We can go out.

               V.B. D'WIT

Batey's lemonade, Wills's cigarettes and Rowntree's chocolates.

Boarding a train at Alresford, it is marvellous just to sit back, relax, and listen to the hiss of steam as you travel through the beautiful Hampshire countryside. First stop is Ropley station, which is famous for the topiary on the bushes on its platforms. This is also the engineering centre of the Mid-Hants Railway.

At some 630ft above sea level, Medstead and Four Marks station is the highest in Southern England. The hills here are so steep that engine crews once remarked that they were "going over the Alps".

Journey's end is at Alton station.

Full steam ahead ... a train on the line between Alresford and Ropley.

ANDREW WOODS

The church of St. Lawrence in Alton was the scene of bitter fighting during the English Civil War. Royalist forces in the town were suddenly attacked by Parliamentarian troops on December 13th, 1643. Led by Sir William Waller, the Roundheads completely surprised the Royalist, Lord Crawford. He set off to find reinforcements in Winchester, leaving only Colonel John Boles and his men to defend Alton.

They did so with great gallantry, but the Parliamentarian forces outnumbered them. The Royalists were

'Rural Rides'   *(continued)*

First stop on the journey is Ropley
Station.   ANDREW WOODS

eventually trapped in St. Lawrence's Church, where they were overpowered. Colonel Boles was killed in the pulpit of the church, though not before he had slain several of the enemy. He was buried at Winchester Cathedral and a brass memorial was erected in his honour. A facsimile in Alton church records the words of Charles I when he heard of the brave Colonel's death: "Bring me a mourning scarf, I have lost one of the best commanders in the kingdom".

Today it is still possible to see bullet holes in the south door of the church. A clay pipe, together with some bullets, are also preserved in a glass case in the church.

Back at Alton station there is time to read the latest leaflet about the Mid-Hants Railway. It gives details of such events as steam enthusiasts' weekends, a morris dancing day and a 1940s weekend. There are even visits by Thomas the Tank Engine and his fellow engines, Henry and James. They are very popular with children who know them from the books by the Reverend W. Awdry. Truly the Watercress Line is a steam railway for all of us to enjoy, whatever our age.

BRYAN R. WOODS

LINCOLN CITY

Organized football has been played in Lincoln since the early 1860s but it was not until 1883 that the present club was formed. Their first success came four years later when they won the Lincolnshire Senior Cup shortly before becoming the first champions of the Midland League. In 1892 they were elected to the newly formed Second Division of the Football League. Two years later the club moved to its present home at Sincil Bank and they stayed at this level until 1920 when they failed to gain re-election. In 1921-22, "The Imps", as they became known, were one of the founder-members of the Third Division North and comfortably held their own at this level. They achieved the championship of this division in 1932 and 1948. Their stay in Division Two was brief on each occasion, but after winning another championship (1951-52) when they scored 121 goals, they had a longer spell in the Second Division, lasting until 1961. Since that time they have often had to endure periods of struggle in the League's basement. Their record in the FA Cup has also been modest, as the last time they reached the equivalent of the fifth round of this competition was back in 1902.

ALAN ROBINSON

Lincoln City (1947-48):

Back row (left to right): J. Grummett, G. Stillyards, T. Johnson, G. Moulsen, R. Owen, A. Bean.
Front row: J. McCormick, J. Hutchinson, A. Lester, H. Parr, W. Windle.

Maurice Chevalier... *and a cocktail of French favourites!*

If ever there was a show business award for the person who made the biggest jump "from rags to riches", then it would surely have to be given to Maurice Chevalier, the world's most famous French entertainer.

Born in a slum district of Paris in September 1888, Maurice was nothing more than a back-street urchin, but he quickly learnt how to earn a living. He extracted several centimes from people by, firstly, doing a few acrobatic antics on street corners to attract their interest (plus cash!) and then — aged only 12 — by singing lusty old songs to people strolling along some of the more fashionable boulevards of the French capital. His upturned hat was always strategically placed on the pavement to catch their eye — and their modest donations ... *"merci beaucoup, monsieur".*

However, it was from that kind of street-wise experience that his near seventy years of show business notoriety sprang forth. By his later teenage years he had developed an appreciative following through putting on song and dance routines in some of the Parisian street cafes and low-level music halls. Then in 1908, while performing at a pavement café, he was spotted by one of France's best-known singing dancers, the saucy and leggy Mistinguette, who added Maurice to her string of music hall performers. She it was who persuaded him to adopt a straw hat and cane when carrying out his act, and together the pair appeared regularly on stage at the famous *Folies-Bergere* in Paris until the outbreak of the First World War in August 1914 which put an end to all such jollity.

Maurice immediately joined the French army but was wounded in 1916 and, after being captured by the Germans, spent the next two years in a prisoner-of-war camp until released at the end of hostilities in November 1918. But his time as a prisoner was not entirely wasted, for he learnt how to speak English after being closeted with several British army detainees — and that was the trigger that eventually brought him world-wide fame. His closest pal in the camp was a miner from County Durham, and that's why when recording songs, or appearing in Hollywood "talkies" later on in his life, Maurice's unique Franco-English accent had a peculiar but distinctively Geordie tone about it!

On his release from captivity following the German surrender, Maurice returned to star with Mistinguette at the *Folies-Bergere*, but his own stylish act suddenly began developing so rapidly that they finally parted company and his solo career really took off. He made his first appearance on the London stage in 1919, starring in *"Hullo America"* at the Palace Theatre, and this began his love affair with the British capital which remained his all-time favourite haunt, apart from his native Paris.

Maurice had another love affair at that time with chorus girl Yvonne Vallee who joined him on the Paris stage in a musical song-and-dance act that led to their wedding. But, as with most show-biz couplings then and now, it didn't last very long and they soon divorced. Meanwhile, Maurice constantly criss-crossed the Channel for almost the next ten years, strutting and dancing across the stage in both environments while twinkling his eyes, shrugging his shoulders and singing those perky songs until Hollywood beckoned the

△ *Maurice appeared in a cigarette card series featuring various MGM film stars in the early Thirties.*

straw-hatted star in 1928. He spent the next seven years over there, making a total of twelve musical films for Paramount, which soon helped to increase his reputation as France's most unique international performer. His first major movie was *"Innocents in Paris"* (1929) which was one of the first talkies ever made and

(continued)

gave birth to his famous signature tune, *"Louise"*:

> Every little breeze seems to whisper
> Louise,
> Birds in the trees seem to twitter
> Louise.
> Each little rose tells me it knows
> I love you, love you ... Louise.

Maurice went on to make a total of some 44 films, many for the Walt Disney corporation later on, but it was his recorded hit songs and one-man shows that remained longest in

the memory of audiences throughout the world. He starred on stage with the famous Dolly Sisters during the early Thirties, and in 1932 he also scored his first big cinema hit with *"Love Me Tonight"* co-starring Jeanette Macdonald and Myrna Loy, which included such vocal treasures as *"Mimi"* and *"Isn't it Romantic?"*

Maurice returned to France in the early summer of 1939 and was trapped there following the outbreak of the Second World War in September. He remained there quietly during the German occupation, mainly in the Vichy section of southern France where the local authorities ruled by collaboration with the Nazis. Maurice used the time to write his memoirs which eventually amounted to eleven separate volumes! It was published in 1946 under the collective title of *"Ma Route et Mes Chansons"* which means "My Way and My Songs".

When the Allies stormed across France and liberated Continental Europe after five years of German control, Maurice quickly got his act together and made a wildly successful world tour of one-man shows — still wearing his straw hat, bow tie, and carrying a cane — even though he was then 58. Indeed, when he was 62 he broke the record for appearances at the Theatre of Varieties, Paris, by

◁ *Like Maurice Chevalier, Edith Piaf — known as the "Little Sparrow" — also began her career as a singer on the streets of Paris.*

making 131 consecutive nightly performances. He carried on working in show business and films — including the award-winning musical *"Gigi"* in 1958 when he was 70 — before eventually retiring in 1968 on reaching his 80th birthday. He was awarded a special Oscar by Hollywood for his outstanding life-long career and made his farewell speech at the Champs-Elysees theatre in Paris before an invited audience which included many international celebrities.

Deprived of his passion for the stage, Maurice only lasted a further three years before dying as a lonely old man in Paris on New Year's Day, 1972, aged 83. But his unique style lives on in a treasure trove of outstanding records.

Another French singer who had a similar upbringing in life to that of Maurice Chevalier, was **Edith Piaf** (1915-1963). Also born in a poor part of Paris, her real name was Edith Gassion but because of her tiny size and high-pitched voice she was dubbed "La Piaf" which is a Parisian slang word for a sparrow, but the name stuck throughout her musical career. Her mother — a street vagrant — had deserted her as a baby and she spent her childhood living with her grandmother in the country.

At the tender age of 14 she returned to Paris and lived with her father, a circus acrobat. She later began tour-

Jeanette Macdonald

ing with him and, to earn a living, Edith began singing on the streets. She was later befriended by Parisian cabaret owner Louis Leplee and he gave her a chance to appear on stage. The audiences loved her deeply emotional style of singing and she quickly became a sensation with the French public and a growing audience of international admirers.

Among her biggest hit songs is her signature tune *"La Vie en Rose"*, for

(continued overleaf)

(continued)

which she also wrote the lyrics. Despite her climb to fame, however, she never enjoyed good health at any time in her life and, after collapsing on stage in 1960, she defied medical advice to give up her exhausting career and died in October 1963, aged only 47.

Jean Sablon was another male singer who, like Maurice Chevalier, appeared as a teenager with the infamous Mistinguette. Born in March 1906, the son of a well-known Parisian theatre orchestra conductor and composer of operettas, he switched from singing classical arias to more modern

△ Charles Trenet, the tenor who composed his own theme song "La Mer" in 1945.

Singer Jean Sablon became known as the "French Bing Crosby".

numbers as the jazzy Twenties progressed and he soon became known as "the French Bing Crosby".

Sablon was in America when war broke out in 1939 and he stayed there throughout the conflict. Among his best-known numbers are the famous *"Sur la Pont, d'Avignon"* which readily conjures up the unique style of French music. He also made several records with the highly-rated Django Reinhardt, the Belgian jazz guitarist, who together with violinist Stephane Grappelli co-founded the famous quintet known as "The Hot Club of France" in 1934.

When microphones became part of the essential equipment for modern dance bands and singers, it was

inevitable that some performers would take to them better than others. Just such a one was **Charles Trenet**, born at Narbonne on France's Mediterranean coast, in May 1913. He became known as a poet and lyric writer, creating some 500 songs during his active life, and later began recording many of them with dance bands of the day. He showed great talents with his use of the microphone, and his clarity of tone attracted a following in the Thirties from old and young listeners alike. Among his best-remembered numbers are "*Boum*" (1938) and "*La Mer*" (1945) which turned out to be his biggest hit song. Both are contained on our latest release. So fill up your glass, sit down and enjoy a taste of *Evergreen's* very special "French Cocktail"!

PERCY BICKERDYKE

Conducted by Mr. Percy Bickerdyke, assisted by Miss Daisy Drummond

GOOD KING WENCESLAS...
IN WARTIME

John Davey of Michigan remembers this yuletide version of the Czech king while a boy during the wartime London Blitz. It was a time when many songs were cleverly parodied and this is both sarcastic and amusing. There must be at least two more verses, possibly more, so can anyone finish it for him?

> Good King Wenceslas looked out
>   on the Feast of Stephen
> When the sirens warbled out,
>   on a note uneven:
> Loudly roared the guns that night,
>   the barrage was a snorter;
> When the warden came in sight,
>   carrying sand and water.
>
> "Hither stooge come stand by me
>   if you know your telling,
> Have you got a stirrup pump
>   handy in your dwelling?"
> "Sire there's sand out round the bend,
>   higher than a mountain,
> We can work the stirrup pump
>   from St. Agnes Fountain."

NATIONAL SOUND ARCHIVE

John Gomer has pointed out this has moved and now resides at the British Library, 96 Euston Road, London NW1 2DB, not the address given in our Autumn issue. It is a national institution so why not make use of it?

It is doubtful if this wartime fireman's hose was connected to the St. Agnes Fountain (see "Good King Wenceslas").

THE TATTOOED LADY

We have been reliably informed that the words relating to the wartime song about the kangaroo in our last issue are unprintable. It seems it was very popular with the soldiers and had a variety of words to suit every occasion. It was called *The Tattooed Lady* and the mind boggles as to what else she might have had imprinted across her anatomy.

DOES THIS SONG HAVE A NAME?

E. Budgen of East Grinstead in Sussex remembers his elderly neighbour singing this song to him more than 70 years ago. The tune is *Believe me if all those endearing young charms*, but does this real tear jerker have a title? One wonders if it is also Irish in origin?

Before the bright sun rises over the hill
In the cornfield poor Mary is seen
In patience her little blue apron to fill
With a few scattered ears she can
    glean.

Poor girl hard at work in the heat of
    the sun
How tired and worn you must be
Why don't you leave off as the
    others have done
And sit with them under the tree?

Oh no, for my mother lies ill in her
    bed
Too feeble to spin or to knit
My two little brothers are crying for
    bread
And I hardly can give them a bit.

How could I sit lazy and idle as they
While they are so hungry and ill?
Oh no, for I'd sooner work hard all
    the day
My little blue apron to fill.

**Magical Music Hall Memories with
your favourite stars of yesterday**

★ Florrie Forde ★ Eugene Stratton ★ Ella Shields
★ George Robey ★ G. H. Elliott ★ Marie Lloyd
★ Charles Coburn ★ Ella Retford ★ Billy Merson
★ Harry Champion

"Signora" was sung by Billy Merson, one of many music hall items on our CD/cassette above. He also sings that well-known favourite "The Spaniard who blighted my life". Oh yes? Oh no! Our free Music and Shop Window catalogues are available on request.

SENOR, SIGNOR SENORA, OR SIGNORA?

The answer is *Signora* (see Autumn issue) and some of you quite rightly pointed out that it is sung by Billy Merson on our CD/cassette "Playing the Halls" C09/E09. A modern cassette version of the song by the Oldham Tinkers was kindly supplied by Jean Gee of St. Helens. Part of the rhyme goes:

If your father "Spaghetti" won't give
    his consent
And says that you can't marry me
I will start a vendetta
And stick my stilleta
In a nice little place he will never
    forgetta ...

*Sounds painful to me. Ouch! — P.B.

Search for a Song...

(continued)

DAVID AND GOLIATH

We are pleased to print the full version of an amusing rhyme about David and Goliath which can be sung to several hymn tunes, including *Hanover*. It was something of a party piece but to be sung deadpan with a lisp as exemplified by William Brown's female acquaintance, the awful Violet Elizabeth.

Goliath of Gath with hith helmet of
    bwath,
Wath theated one day upon the
    gween gwath,
When up thlipped thlim David, the
    thervant of Thaul
And thaid I will thmite thee, though I
    am tho thmall.

Smooth stones fwom the bwook,
    thlim David then took
And made him a thling with pietheth
    of thwing,
And with hith thuthpender he made
    thoth thones fly
And hit old Goliath a thmack in the
    eye.

Goliath he thwore and thuthwith he
    thpake
Blank, blank, blank, blank, blank,
    blank blankety blank.
The air all awound him woth turning
    quite blue
He thwore all the old wordth and
    then thwore some new.

Goliath then fell in a thwoon on the
    thward
Then up thlipped thlim David and
    pulled out hith thword.
He stood on Goliath and chopped off
    hith head
And all Ithwael thouted, "Goliath ith
    dead!"

Aaaa-rd luck (instead of Amen!)

In the 1977 TV series, Adrian Dannatt was William Brown and Bonnie Langford a young Violet Elizabeth who threatened to "Scweam and scweam till I'm thick!".

QUICKY REQUESTS

Does anyone know *Auntie Maud's Shawl* an old song which began:

> My Auntie Maud had a beautiful shawl

and ends:

> When the butcher's not looking, the fat for the cooking, goes into my Auntie Maud's shawl.

— MRS. M. NOONAN, 5 YULANDA PLACE, ORANGE 2800, AUSTRALIA.
It sounds like the opposite to Corporal Jones's shop in "Dad's Army". — P.B.

Could someone supply me with the full version of a song which begins:

> I work in a London bank, a respectable position ...

— BRENDA WARNER, 21 HARTLAND ROAD, EPPING, ESSEX, CM16 4PF.
Daisy thinks it is part of the 1953 Guy Mitchell hit song She wears red feathers *and a huly-huly skirt but we cannot find the words. — P.B.*

Can anyone help me with the words of the song *I only want to be a barrow boy*?
— T. CLAYTON, 68 HUNT ROAD, HIGHAM LANE, TONBRIDGE, KENT, TN10 4BG.

I am looking for a cassette of a song called *Serenata* which begins:

> Like a golden dream it is carried in my heart ...

— T.W. GOWERS, 118 PYMS ROAD, GALLEYWOOD, CHELMSFORD, ESSEX, CM2 8QA.

I hope that some of your readers can help me with the words and music of a

Guy Mitchell was an American but a devoted Anglophile who toured both Britain and Australia. Among his many hit songs was "She wears red feathers" from 1953, and which a reader is trying to locate.

song which my father sang during the 1920s. He was a music hall artiste called Bert Hague, "Yorkshire's Singing Pit Lad" and I wish to include it in some reminiscences I am writing for my grandson. It is called *The hand that rocks the cradle rules the world.* — JACK CODMAN, 11 DUNSTER DRIVE, SULLY, PENARTH, GLAMORGAN, CF64 5TN.

Does anyone know my father's party piece, an Irish nonsense rhyme?

> Down in Kilkenny what a noise they are making,
> Poor little Jimmy Murphy is the boy they are taking.

— BRIAN BURROWS, 5 WEST WAY, SHIPLEY, YORKSHIRE, BD18 4HW.

Search for a Song...

(continued)

Who sang a song to the tune of Tchaikovsky's *Italian Caprice* and can anyone supply all the words? It starts:

You told the valley of echo that you
    loved me (you loved me)

— PHILIP FOX, 107 LIGHTWATER MEADOW, LIGHTWATER, SURREY, GU18 5XJ.

Following the mention of patriotic songs recently, here is another which I remember. Could it have been linked to the RAF during the war? Who wrote it and has it ever been recorded?

England, our island home,
Land of the free.
Britain unconquered yet
O'er land and sea.
Lord of the heavens above
Answer our prayer,
God keep Britain's sons
Lords of the air.

— ROSINA JONES, 141 GRIMSHAW LANE, MIDDLE-TON JUNCTION, MANCHESTER, M24 2BR.

Was the Battle of Britain, depicted here in an evocative painting by Louis Keene, the inspiration for a wartime song possibly called "England, our island home"?

Enid Blyton's "Noddy" (right) and Big Ears (left) were a huge success with children, despite what the spoilsport politically correct lobby of today might think. Two grandparents would like to locate Noddy tunes to sing to their grandchildren.

Can someone help me find a recording of a song which might have been by John McCormack?

> I dream of the day I met you
> I dream of light divine
> That shone in your tender eyes, love,
> When first they looked in mine.

— HILARY KEEFE, 51A STONE CROSS LANE, LOWTON, WARRINGTON, LANCASHIRE, WA3 2SD.

The following was sung to me by a patient in a nursing home. I believe it is called *Portrait of a Lady* and may have been performed by Jack Daly. Does anyone know all the verses?

> When lights are low at eventide
> I dream of days gone by
> And there's a picture I can see
> Against the evening sky.

— MRS. M. ELDER, 13 ASHCOTT PLACE, BURNHAM-ON-SEA, SOMERSET, TA8 1HN.

Can anyone supply me with the words for what I think is some kind of drinking song? It begins:

> In cellars cool at ease I sit
> Upon a barrel resting ...

— CHARLES COLEMAN, 60 THE STREET, WRECCLESHAM, FARNHAM, SURREY, GU10 4QR.

I should think he probably fell off the barrel if he started drinking from it! — P.B.

When our children were small we loved to sing songs from Enid Blyton's "Noddy" books. One was called *The Toyland Train*:

> Isn't it fun when the Toyland Train
> goes huffing and puffing along ...

And *The Wobbly Man*.

> I push him as hard as ever I can ...

Now we would like to sing them to our grandchildren. Can anyone help us? —
MR. & MRS. STEADMAN, 5 CHIPPERFIELD ROAD, HEMEL HEMPSTEAD, HERTFORDSHIRE, HP3 0AQ.

Snippets from your letters — discussed by Percy Bickerdyke

GOODNIGHT PRETTY MAIDEN

Like most people, I have a habit of always skimming through the death notices in my daily paper and it was with great sadness this autumn that I spotted the demise of a dear old friend with whom I had regularly

exchanged Christmas cards over the years. Her name was Rita, and as well as being a wonderful pianist she was the power behind the throne of her famous singing husband, Cavan O'Connor, the strolling vagabond who won this country's heart on stage for well over sixty years.

Rita, born in June 1907, was the niece of the great operatic diva Dame Maggie Teyte, and her uncle was a renowned composer. It was this musical connection that brought Rita and Cavan together, for both were students at the Royal College of Music in the mid Twenties. They married in 1929 and had three sons, all of whom inherited artistic talents from their parents. One of them, John, is a well-known artist who is currently in Rome painting an official portrait of the Pope.

◁ *Dame Maggie Teyte (1888-1976) the renowned English soprano who was born at Wolverhampton. After being coached in France by Claude Debussy, she had a dazzling operatic career on both sides of the Atlantic.*

Although Cavan — born not in Ireland but at Nottingham in 1899 — was the one in the limelight, appearing on stage, broadcasting and making records, Rita was always close by him in the background, playing the piano for rehearsals at home and accompanying him at charity concerts up and down the country until both were in their eighties.

I last popped in to see them at their Kensington home when Cavan was on the verge of his 93rd birthday (see picture). He died in 1997 and Rita struggled on for a further seven years trying to cope with her loss. What a lovely couple they were, and their melody will certainly linger on.

More 'Percy's Postbag' overleaf ▷

Cavan leans over his wife Rita's shoulder as they practise together, singing and playing at their home in Kensington. They were married for over 67 years.

(continued)

YOKOHAMA OR DUBLIN?

Reader Fred Snape of Woodbridge in Suffolk was delighted with the response to his request printed in our Summer 2004 issue for information about a wartime spoof song called "Yokohama Mama" which he first heard while serving in the RAF in the Libyan desert.

He now writes to tell me that he has had several answers, including tape recordings, from Wales and Canada. The group that recorded the song called themselves "Harry Kari and his six Saki Sippers" and the words — in pidgin English — tell of a man going into a Chinese restaurant and taking a shine to an Oriental waitress who did not reciprocate his feelings.

Oddly enough, our reader now knows that the tune was a mock rendering of that well-known Irish folk song which begins:

In Dublin's fair city,
Where the girls are so pretty,
I first set my eyes on sweet
  Molly Malone.
As she wheeled her wheel barrow
Through streets broad and narrow,
Crying "Cockles and mussels
Alive alive O".

Perhaps its return to popularity is because Chinese restaurants serve cockles and mussels with their egg fried rice dishes these days!

A CUP OF NAAFI TEA

While talking about old wartime songs, reader Cyril Grant of Hamilton (Canada) reminds me of another spoof ditty that was all the rage in my Navy canteen. Can you recall singing this one to the tune of *"Trees"*, a song that was featured in our Spring issue this year?

I think that I shall never see
A drink as weak as NAAFI tea
For when it pours out from the pot
I can't tell if it's tea or not!
The water's there for all to see,
But only God could find the tea!

▽ Evergreen's *CD of Cavan O'Connor, the singing troubador of stage and radio fame. See pages 142-3 for details of ordering.*

Cavan O'Connor
The Strolling Vagabond
Songs by the singing troubador of stage and radio fame

Including:
★ Could You Be True To Eyes Of Blue? ★ Starlight Serenade
★ At The Close Of A Long, Long Day ★ One Alone
★ A Pretty Girl Is Like a Melody
★ When I Leave The World Behind
★ Singing A Vagabond Song
★ God Will Remember ★ Goodnight etc.

Evergreen Melodies

Announcing a new collection of monologues by
Stanley Holloway

Following the best-selling success of the first volume, *Evergreen* and *This England* have now produced a second CD of classic monologues and songs by the great star of stage and screen: Stanley Holloway. Anyone who enjoyed Albert Ramsbottom's encounter with Wallace the lion on the first CD will laugh out loud at the mischievous schoolboy's latest adventures: when he is evacuated, has a ghostly encounter at the Tower of London, and is reunited with his old feline adversary at the zoo. And another of Stanley Holloway's great characters,

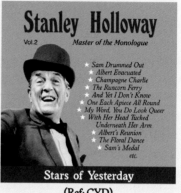

(Ref: CYD)

Sam Small, the stubborn Yorkshire soldier, also makes several comical reappearances: joining the Home Guard, winning a medal, delivering a sturgeon to the king etc.

This new compact disc features a number of other monologues, including that masterpiece of black humour, "My Word, You Do Look Queer", and to add to the variety Stanley Holloway can be heard singing a few famous songs, including "The Floral Dance" and "Champagne Charlie".

As one generation is succeeded by another, the monologues made famous by Stanley Holloway continue to delight everyone who hears them, both young and old. Whether you are only just discovering their unique appeal, or are a life-long fan who can recite some of the words, you'll love this new CD and enjoy listening to its tracks over and over again.

CD PRICE: £8.95 (inc. UK post). Overseas surface mail (airmail in brackets) £10 (£11); or US $18 ($20); Can $24 ($27); Aus $27 ($30); NZ $31 ($34).

 **PO Box 52, Cheltenham, Glos., GL50 1YQ.**

Telephone orders: **01242-515156** *(All major cards accepted)*

There were many authors during the Victorian period who set out to entertain their readers while, at the same time, attempting to instil in them qualities of courage, honesty and resourcefulness in the face of danger, as well as devotion to God, Queen and Country. Such a writer was George Manville Fenn who, though widely read at the time has, today, fallen so far from favour that he even fails to find a place in the *Dictionary of National Biography*. He left no autobiography and, unlike such contemporaries as R.M. Ballantyne (author of *Coral Island*) and W.H.G. Kingston, nobody wrote his biography.

Enough information is available,

The writer that England forgot

however, to bring this undeservedly forgotten writer from the past into the light of day. Born in Pimlico, London, on 3rd January 1831, his education comprised a mixture of home tuition and private schools, followed by three years at St. John's Teachers' Training College in Battersea. Leaving there in 1854, he became Master at the Church of England School in Alford, Lincolnshire. He was there for three years, during which time he married a local girl Susan Leake who, during a long and happy relationship, presented him with two sons and six daughters.

When George decided that teaching was not his calling, the young couple went to London where he studied printing, later turning up, as revealed in a business directory, at Crowle, Lincolnshire, as a printer, publisher and bookseller. He published a small monthly magazine, *Modern Metro*, which survived only from May to September 1862. He next appears as part-proprietor of the *Herts and Essex Observer*.

At last he hit upon the profession which was to bring him fame during his lifetime, for in 1864 he contributed a sketch entitled "In Jeopardy" to *All the Year Round* whose editor was none other than Charles Dickens. This gave him an entry into journalism, and he contributed articles and features to a range of publications. He became editor of *Cassell's Magazine* and took over the ownership of the journal, *Once a Week*, until it closed in 1879.

These were days of versatility, for he was also dramatic critic for *The Echo* for several years and, during the 1880s, wrote no fewer than eight plays, all of which were performed, with reasonable success, on the London stage.

All this varied literary work preceded the appearance of his first juvenile novel, *Hollowdell Grange* (1866), and his debut novel for adults, *Bent Not Broken* (1887). Over the next 30 years these were followed by a remarkable flow of some 170 stories.

A true Victorian, both in appearance and in his writings for young people and adults, George Manville Fenn ranged the world for his subjects.

Apart from his early days in Lincolnshire, Fenn was essentially a southerner, living for a time on a Sussex farm before moving to London Garden Suburb in 1880 and, nine years later, to Syon Lodge, a large house in Isleworth, Middlesex, where he spent the rest of his life.

Unlike many of his contemporaries he never left England and yet his boys' books are often set in exotic situations all over the world, including Australia with *First in the Field* (1894), in which he demonstrates a surprisingly modern attitude to the plight of convicts. *To Win or Die* (1904) sees Fenn in his most dramatic

(continued)

mood with a tale of the Yukon, while, in sharp contrast, *Jungle and Stream* (1898) follows the lively adventures of two boys in Thailand.

In all his boys' stories (girls rarely have a look in!) Fenn had a definite aim in mind, as he explained in a rare press interview with the *Boy's Own Paper* in 1904:

I find that what my boys throughout the world like best is a good tale of adventure — pure, wholesome, breathing the true British spirit, and showing goals attained by bulldog perseverance, patience and pluck.

Fenn may have been a Londoner, but he never forgot his early days in Lincolnshire, for one of his best stories was *Dick o' the Fens* (1888), which, almost foretelling today's environmental concerns, features the clash between the landowners who intend to drain the Fens to provide more farm-land and the Fenmen who will lose their traditional right to cut reeds for thatching, catch fish and trap ducks for market.

The author's own experiences also shine through *Brownsmith's Boy* (1886) in which the young hero learns the market gardener's trade, not without many ups and downs, including a colourful description of a trip by horse and cart to sell strawberries at Covent Garden. Fenn himself had a six-acre garden stocked with fruit trees and vegetables of every description, and sold

◁ *An exciting scene from "New Forest Spy", typical of Fenn's belief that his readers loved tales of adventure and danger.*

the surplus at the famous London market.

He deployed the same meticulous care in plot and background in all his other home-based tales, whether they were located in the West Country, as in *Devon Boys* (1887); the Peak District, *Will of the Mill* (1903); or the Scottish Highlands, with *Three Boys* (1889).

No less wide-ranging were his overseas stories, such as *Nat the Naturalist* (1883), in which a man introduces his nephew Nat to the wonderful flora and fauna of Sumatra, Java, Celebes, Borneo and New Guinea. He shows the same attention to accuracy in his army stories, and is quite prepared to bring the reality of war to his young readers as is evident from the titles of such stories as *Draw Swords!* (1889), a tale of the Bengal Horse Artillery, and *Shoulder Arms* (1905).

His sea stories are equally atmospheric and *Sail Ho!* (1893), a gripping tale of a mutiny at sea, is as good a story as any he wrote. Not far behind in excitement are such titles as *Hunting the Skipper* (1906), a story recounting the voyage of the Navy in the days of sail, and *Middy and Ensign* (1883), which tells of the rivalry of a midshipman and a young army ensign whose unit is bound for a post on the Malay coast on board a steam-powered vessel.

This, however, is no more than a brief glimpse of his wide-ranging books for boys, which also include

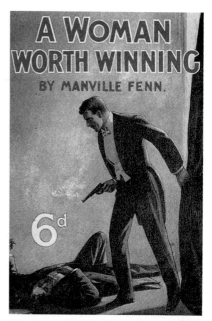

The illustrated cover of "A Woman Worth Winning" prepared readers for the dramatic events recounted in its pages.

historical tales such as *In Honour's Cause* (1896) set, unusually, in the reign of George II. There were school stories, like *Burr Junior* (1891), and tales of exploration and natural disasters, of which *Fire Island* (1894) is both unusual and thrilling. He wrote several stories about smugglers, including *Cutlass and Cudgel* (1890), while he was not afraid to air his anti-slavery opinions in *Mass' George* (1890).

If Fenn's stories for young people cover a wide area of time and place, his adult novels similarly range over many different occupations and backgrounds, from the latest engineering

'The Literary Pilgrim'

(continued)

One of Fenn's most exciting novels, "Coming Home to Roost", was set amongst the slate mines of North Wales. This quarry is at Blaenau Ffestiniog.

MIKE COWEN

techniques of his day to mining and quarrying. He explores many aspects of Victorian society, unearthing some of its less-commendable features as well as the virtues which we ascribe to the period. In the process, he shows a remarkable knowledge of the technology, the commercial practices, the social tensions and the international rivalries of his day.

His backgrounds are etched in with quite remarkable technical accuracy, thanks, no doubt, to the contents of his extraordinary library. For example, *The White Virgin* (1894) features a derelict tin mine in the Peak District, which two rival parties, one good, one evil, both believe can be restored to profitability by modern mining methods, quite expertly described by Fenn in one of his most exciting adult tales which has an ingenious twist at the end. Rivalry on an international scale forms the background of *An Electric Spark* (1895) when competing interests fight over the mastery of an innovative marine power plant, with a web of espionage and skulduggery woven round Fenn's remarkable knowledge of the technology that was involved.

He is not afraid to spotlight the growing struggle between employers and unions. This is the background of *The Parson O' Dunford* (1879) in which the young parson of the title is not averse to using physical violence to protect an employer against his rebellious workers. Diving and under-water activity is another of Fenn's lit-erary enthusiasms and one of the best of several novels on this theme is *Coming Home to Roost* (1904), set in the North Wales slate mining area where a young diving contractor finds himself involved in a local feud which almost costs him his life.

Appropriately, perhaps, his last novel, *Jack the Rascal* (1909), was writ-ten for the young folk whose tastes he knew so well. This was published posthumously, for it was written sometime before his very last book, his biography of G.A. Henty, complet-ed in 1907. After a long illness, he died on 20th August, 1909, and was buried in Isleworth cemetery.

Today, when there is a healthy interest in reprinting some of the works of out-of-print Victorian writ-ers, George Manville Fenn surely deserves a place in the list. While awaiting the revival, it is worthwhile contacting members of the book-search fraternity who are usually able to locate the best-known titles. It will prove a rewarding exercise and a worthy memorial to a notable repre-sentative of all that was best in Victorian literature. ERIC FORD

Rural Recipes *Old English Cider Cake*

Ingredients:

2 eggs
4 oz butter
4 oz caster sugar
8 oz plain flour
1 teaspoon baking powder
½ grated nutmeg
5 fl oz cider

Method:
Beat the eggs over a pan of warm water. Cream the butter and sugar until fluffy and beat in the eggs gradually. Sieve the flour and baking powder and fold into the mixture. Add the nutmeg and cider. Transfer the mixture to a 9-inch sand-wich tin lined with greaseproof paper. Bake in a moderately hot oven (190°C, 375°F, gas mark 5) for 20 minutes.

From: **The National Trust & West Country Tourist Board's Book of Afternoon Tea** by Marika Hanbury Tenison, published by David & Charles.

I awoke early to a bitterly cold day. There was a deep chill in the blankets and the ice lay thick on the window pane. I shivered in my bed. It was December 1938 in the Lancashire of the Depression and there were many men unemployed, including my father. I had watched him every day putting fresh newspaper in his shoes to cover the holes in the soles before tramping the streets looking for work.

Today was Christmas Eve and, although we had no money, as a four-year-old child I was excited. I got out of bed and joined my mother in the living room. She was sitting beside an empty fireplace, softly weeping. We had no coal, no money and very little food.

Later that day my father came

A miracle at Christmas

home with a few shillings which bought some sausages, potatoes and bread for tomorrow's festive dinner. When he was told that the local parish church was helping people who had children, he went along. At first he was refused help because he didn't attend regularly, but when the vicar heard that I went to the Sunday school he gave my father a rag doll for me and a slab of Christmas cake, for which he had to get on his knees and pray.

While my father was at the church, my mother had a caller. It was Mr. Travis who was an agent for some kind of credit club my mother paid into. She was upset and ashamed that she was unable to pay him the two shillings. Mr. Travis was a kind man who used to give me a ship halfpenny

Can You Name These Stars?

This picture from the late-Forties shows a famous film star with his two daughters, both of whom also became well-known film stars. The older daughter first appeared as a baby in the Noel Coward film *In Which We Serve* while the younger daughter starred with her father in a dramatic 1959 film set in South Wales. She also played twins in a Hollywood tear jerker. Can you name all three, plus their famous mother and any of the films alluded to? Check your answers on page 101.

every week, so he told her not to worry.

That evening my mother sat me down and, with sadness in her voice and tears in her eyes, told me that Santa would not be coming to me that night. She explained that there had been no money to send to him, and we didn't even have enough coal and not much food. I remember asking her why she didn't pray to God for food and coal. We were told in Sunday school that if you asked God, He would provide. I wasn't concerned about Santa not coming as surely my mother was mistaken. Santa came to every child, didn't he?

I got down on my knees and prayed to God to stop my mother crying,

(continued overleaf)

A jovial butcher stands proudly beside his festive window display at Otley in the West Riding of Yorkshire.

CLIFFORD ROBINSON

and to please bring us coal and food; then I went to bed. I awoke next morning to see a half-filled pillowcase at the end of my bed as I knew I would. I could hear the fire crackling and when I went into the living room there was the table set for breakfast with a bowl of fruit in the centre.

"I told you! I told you!" I shrieked, "that God would provide if you asked Him!"

My mother started to cry again, but this time with joy. She exchanged looks with my father, who whispered "Out of the mouths of babes".

A miracle happened that Christmas in the form of a real Santa, Mr. Travis. I learned many years later that, when he got home, he was very concerned about us as he knew things must be really bad for my mother to be unable to pay him. He felt guilty that his family had so much while ours had so little. So, late on Christmas Eve, he arrived with his wife armed with all the essentials of Christmas including coal for the fire and toys for me.

I treasured my rag doll, which my mother scrubbed and painted a new face on for many years. She would never let me discard it as she said it reminded her to always count her blessings in future years.

SARAH MAY ALFORD

Don't miss out on
A Treasury of THIS ENGLAND

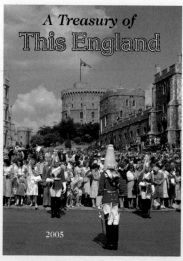

A Treasury of This England

2005

Size: 10" x 7½"   144 pages

Ever since it was first launched almost 40 years ago, *This England* magazine has been at the forefront of a campaign to revive the love for Shakespeare's "sceptred isle" by publishing articles about our nation's rich heritage, countryside, culture and traditions. During that time, readers all over the world have enjoyed a vast array of fascinating stories, stunning photographs and beautiful poetry celebrating the English way of life.

This new hardback book brings together a selection of some of the very best material from the early years of publication, with articles about famous literary figures, curious customs, the seasons of the year etc. — enough, in fact, to please everyone. In many cases, the original articles have been improved by the addition of new, full-colour illustrations, producing a lavish, high-quality book that will never go out of date. The **Treasury of This England** (144 pages, hardback, size: 10" x 7½") makes a perfect Christmas gift for family and friends at home or abroad who love our green and pleasant land. See also page 112 in this issue.

Price: **£14.95** inc. UK p&p.
Overseas surface mail (airmail in brackets): **£17** (£22) or
US $34 ($44); Canada $45 ($58); Australia $46 ($59);
New Zealand $53 ($68).

This England
PO Box 52, Cheltenham, Gloucestershire, GL50 1YQ

Tel: **01242-515156**   *All major cards accepted*

CINEMAGIC

The best bargain I ever had was paying fourpence to see the movie *King Kong*. I was 18 and had just started my National Service at RAF Padgate, near Warrington in Lancashire.

I was instantly hooked. Like *Gone With the Wind*, almost everyone has seen the original *King Kong*. It has been on world-wide television more than any film except *The Wizard of Oz*.

The leading lady was Fay Wray who died in August this year at the age of 96. The scenes of the giant ape climbing to the top of the Empire State Building with the screaming actress clutched in his paw must be among the most memorable in cinema history.

It was ludicrous hokum of course, but it was brilliantly made with tremendous special effects and the film is still gripping today.

Most people think that Fay Wray made just this one film. In fact, she made 77 pictures and that's not counting early walk-on parts in silent films.

She was born, Vina Fay Wray, in 1907, her father Canadian, her mother American. When she was small the family moved from Alberta, Canada, to her mother's home town, Salt Lake City. Fay's parents separated — she never quite found out why — and she was brought up by her mother.

When Fay was 14, Mrs. Wray sent her to live in sunny Los Angeles, with a family friend, fearing that another hard Utah winter would damage her frail daughter's health.

The friend knew people working in Hollywood's infant film industry and before she left school Fay was an extra in silent pictures. After appearing in various Westerns, she starred in *The Wedding March* (1928). This was followed by pictures including *Legion of the Condemned* (1928), with Gary Cooper, and *The Four Feathers* (1929).

She was 25 when the producer-

Fay Wray — King Kong's leading lady

director Merian Cooper chose her to play Ann Darrow in *King Kong* (1933). He told her that her next film would team her with the "tallest, darkest leading man in Hollywood". Fay thought he meant Cary Grant and almost pulled out when she learned the leading man was a 50-foot gorilla!

But she was a game girl and carried on. For most of the shooting of the film, Kong was an 18-inch-high jointed model covered in rabbit hair and shot against miniaturised backgrounds to make him look enormous. A giant Kong hand and head (each eye was a foot across and two men sat inside to work the ferocious grin) were also constructed.

The hand was fitted on a hydraulic lift and for many shots Fay had the giant fingers wrapped around her, and was hoisted 10 feet into the air. As she screamed and struggled, the grip of the fingers loosened and there were many times when she almost fell out. The part was physically demanding in other ways too. Fay hung from ropes, yards from the ground. She floundered in swamps and, on one occasion, Cooper kept her working for 22 hours non-stop.

King Kong took 10 months to shoot, but most of the time was spent on the special effects. Kong was activated by the stop-action technique: the little model was moved a fraction of an inch, one frame of film was shot, the model was given another tiny movement, another frame was shot.

Although she appeared in over 70 films, Fay Wray was best known for her role in "King Kong".

When the film was run at normal speed, the big ape walked, bent down and beat his chest. This film was then back-projected onto a screen and Fay and the rest of the cast were filmed in front of it, so they appeared to be interacting with Kong.

In fact, Fay Wray was filming for only 10 weeks of the 10 months and was paid for just the weeks she worked. She earned $10,000 (worth about £2,500 in those days). Stars today are normally paid "residuals",

(continued overleaf)

'Cinemagic'

(continued)

Fay was told she would be playing opposite the "tallest, darkest leading man in Hollywood", little realising he was an ape!

meaning that each time their film is shown in cinemas or on television, they earn a proportion of their original salary.

"If I'd had residuals in my contract for *Kong* I'd be very rich indeed," Fay said 50 years after the film was first shown, "but then I'd probably not be such a nice person."

Everyone who worked with or met Fay commented on her niceness. Cary Grant told a friend it was just as well he didn't marry her. His pernickety nature made her too good for him.

After *King Kong*, Fay tended to be typecast as the blonde in danger and she wasn't happy with the situation. She came to England to try to change it, making three films in 1935. The first, *Bulldog Jack*, was with Jack Hulbert, the second, *The Clairvoyant*, with Claude Rains, the third, *Come Out of the Pantry*, with Jack Buchanan.

It didn't work. Back in Hollywood all that people remembered were Fay's terrified screams when Kong molested her. (She was actually shut in a recording studio and made to scream, shriek and whimper for 10 minutes. The distressing sounds were dubbed into the film as needed.)

Fay married three times: first to the brilliant screenwriter John Monk Saunders who wrote the classic early aviation picture *Wings* (1927). Sadly he treated his wife very badly and they later divorced.

Her second husband was another screenwriter, Robert Riskin. He had written some important films including *It Happened One Night* (1934), starring Clark Gable, which was hugely influential in changing the style of romantic comedy in Hollywood. Riskin also wrote *Lost Horizon* (1937), *Mr. Deeds Goes to Town* (1936), *Platinum Blonde* (1931) and *You Can't Take it With You* (1938).

Soon after he met Fay in 1941, Riskin came to Britain to help Ed Murrow with his broadcasts to America from wartime London.

Fay and Robert were happy for a decade before he suffered a stroke. She gave up her career to nurse him for the next five years until his death.

After Riskin's death, she made another seven or eight pictures and worked in television.

In 1971 she married her third husband, Dr. Sandy Rothenburg, who had treated Robert Riskin during his illness.

Fay had three children, a son and two daughters, and most of her long life was happy and joyful. Well into her eighties she was still talking and writing about *King Kong*. In her nineties she was driving her car about Los Angeles and was described as "America's oldest celebrity".

Though Fay worked with the biggest stars — Gary Cooper, Cary Grant, Clark Gable, Ronald Colman and Spencer Tracy — she never really became a major star herself. But because of that image of the tiny blonde and the huge ape, she will always be remembered. As a tribute, the Empire State Building — on which Kong died and Fay cowered in the film — dimmed its lights for 15 minutes on the evening of her death.

FRANK JEFFERY

Martian Love Song

"Your eyes have won me over,
They're so wonderful to view,
For one is brown, and one is green,
And the other three are blue!"

JOHN ROBERTSON

RE ARE YOU NOW ••• WHERE ARE YOU NOW ••• WHERE

Have you lost contact with a dear friend? Is there a close relative from whom you haven't heard for many years? Or perhaps you're trying to trace an old wartime sweetheart to see how they have fared in the intervening years ... As people change jobs, get married, move house, or maybe even start new lives on the other side of the world, it is all too easy for addresses to be lost and for individuals to drift apart. Through the pages of this regular feature we hope to be able to help *Evergreen* readers in their search for that lost person or family. Happily, a number of friends have already been reunited as a result of letters being published in previous issues.

Requests, with a photograph where possible, should be sent to "Where are you now?", *Evergreen*, PO Box 52, Cheltenham, Glos. GL50 1YQ, and include any relevant background information: the person's age, last-known residence, occupation, marital status, etc. We receive a large amount of mail so it is impossible for us to publish or acknowledge receipt of every letter. To improve your chances please try to make your requests as interesting as you can, while at the same time remaining concise. Due to pressure on space we must restrict the service to those with whom all contact has been lost for at least 20 years.

WARTIME LETTER

When Jon Mills of Cheltenham in Gloucestershire was taking apart an old dresser he had bought at auction earlier this year, an envelope that had been stuck at the back of one of the drawers came flying out and fell on the floor. The envelope, which was going yellow with age, was addressed to 1739544 Gunner Hunt, Room B214, No.7 Troop, B Battery, 217th S/L T.R.R.A, Bradbury Lines, Hereford.

Inside was a letter from "Prue" to her husband "Hubert". On three pages, written neatly in ink, she laments the fact that he had been unable to get a pass, worries about whether things will ever return to normal after the war, and proclaims her love for him. At the end of the letter she says that "Prudence", presumably their baby daughter, "has been a bit exhausting".

Mr. Mills is anxious that the letter should be returned to Hubert, Prue or Prudence. Are they still around? Does anybody know where they are? If so, please let *Evergreen* know!

SPECIAL AUNT

SIR: My very special aunt, Elizabeth Watkins, died a few months ago and I would like to know if anyone has any old photos of her. During World War II she was in the WRENS and served in a communications unit in Northern Ireland for part of the time, never divulging the nature of her work. She was known as Liz Reddington then.

Afterwards she married and went to live in New Zealand, finding life hard as she studied for a teaching diploma whilst being a wife and mother to her four children.

A patriotic soul who served her homeland well, I feel she should not be forgotten. Her favourite hymn was *I Vow To Thee My Country*. — MARGARET KENNEDY, 16 ST. ANDREW'S GARDENS, BLACKHILL, CONSETT, DURHAM DH8 8RY.

Did you know Elizabeth Watkins (1924-2004) who served in the WRENS as Liz Reddington? See letter on this page.

SHOE SHOP FRIEND

SIR: I emigrated to Australia in 1951, a few years after my husband died, and lost touch with a new Polish friend, Irene Lozovic. We first met at Skinner's Shoe Shop in Hammersmith, London, where she was buying "Start-rite" footwear for her little girl, Bosha.

Irene was separated from her husband at that time and he had gone to live in Argentina. I am now 83 years of age and not in the best of health. I do not know how much time I have left to live on this earth, and would dearly love to hear from Irene, Bosha, or any other members of their family. — MRS. CATHERINE FAIRFAX, 10 HAYDEN AVENUE, FRANKSTON, VICTORIA, AUSTRALIA 3199.

SCOTTISH ARTIST

SIR: As a young constable in the West Australia Police I worked in Geraldton, north of Perth, in the 1960s. My flatmate for a time was an artist from Scotland called Allan MacLean. When he moved on he gave me a lovely water-colour painting of an early type of lobster boat tied up at the local wharf. I would now like to donate this to the Geraldton Maritime Museum as it shows a little piece of history: the boat subsequently sank and the wharf has been demolished. The artist may know more about the vessel he painted, but I have no idea of his present whereabouts. Can anyone help? — VIC HARRIS, 10 GIFFORD WAY, DIANELLA, PERTH, WESTERN AUSTRALIA 6059.

Lily Olive Heed (right) was the best of friends with Tess Dallison (left) before Lily moved from Surrey, England, to Surrey in Canada. See letter below.

ATS TESS

SIR: I am trying to trace an old ATS buddy of mine. Her name was Esther Dallison, but she was known as Tess. She lived in Redhill, Surrey, where her father worked at Monotype.

With her sister Joan I was bridesmaid to Tess when she married Ken Davis from Wales in October 1946. The last time I heard from her was in the 1950s when she had two children, Dianne and Nicky. She may have more now.

Tess is on the left of the photo above, and I am on the right. She is a few years younger than me and I am now 75.

Any help anyone can give me to find her will be greatly appreciated. — LILY OLIVE HEED, NUMBER 72, 2120 KING GEORGE HIGHWAY, SURREY, BRITISH COLUMBIA, CANADA V4A 6Y8.

TREVOR AND BETTY

SIR: My late husband Bob was in the 3rd Ack-Ack Tractor Battery Royal Artillery 1940-46, mainly stationed in Gloucester. He made a firm friendship with Trevor Williams from Blaengwynfi, near Port Talbot, South Wales. The photo below was taken in the garden of our home near Watford, Hertfordshire, when Trevor was on demob leave. With him are his wife Betty and young son Colin. They later had another son called David.

I would be more than pleased to have current news of these lovely people, who are probably unaware that my Bob died in 2001. — MRS. P.D. JOHNSON, 6 RAYFORD COURT, BUCKHURST ROAD, BEXHILL ON SEA, SUSSEX, TN40 1QE.

Betty and Trevor Williams in 1946 with their first son Colin. See letter above.

HOLLIES GIRLS

SIR: I am looking for Margaret Harrison who married David Fletcher and had four sons. My husband and I last saw her when we were in Europe in 1969.

Margaret and I both attended the Hollies Convent in Manchester. We lived very close to each other at one time. Then her parents moved a few miles away to Didsbury and I travelled further afield with my folks to South Africa. If anyone knows where she is now, I would like to be in contact with Margaret again. — HANNA COLLINS (née DUNICZ), PO BOX 12506, JACOBS, 4026, SOUTH AFRICA.

PALLADIUM CONCERT

SIR: In the late 1920s the dancing school I attended was invited to take part in a Sunday afternoon concert at the famous London Palladium Theatre. I had a partner by the name of Roger. Many stage stars of that era were also involved. I remember the infamous Fan Dancers: not because of their lack of clothing, but due to the fact that I was allowed to stroke one of the fans.

The event was in aid of those who had been wounded in World War I. I have often wondered how many of the other performers kept their memento as I did. It is in the form of a soldier depicted on a lapel badge, and there were many men wearing the blue uniform in the audience. One was in a bed, with a little dog sitting on top, which stayed quietly with his master throughout the proceedings.
— MAUREEN EDSON, 16 ELSMORE CRESCENT, PAKURANGA, AUCKLAND 1706, NEW ZEALAND.

If you have a World War I Concert Party commemorative lapel badge like this one, Maureen Edson would like to hear from you. See letter on this page.

A GOOD COOK

SIR: May Evans is the name of a very good cook I met during the Hitler war. We were both stationed at Patrington in East Yorkshire, although she was a native of Long Eaton, on the borders of Derbyshire and Nottinghamshire.

I was a waitress in the WAAF and my nickname was "Wooley" which was taken from my surname. Even though the world was enduring a time of conflict, May and I shared some happy days together. It would be good to relive them, but our lives went separate ways and I lost touch with her. — MRS. DORA WHALEN (née WOOLSTON), FLAT 8, PARK ROAD, LOWESTOFT, SUFFOLK NR32 1SW.

There is something triumphant and enduring about the play *Peter Pan*. It was written by Sir James Matthew Barrie (1860-1937) the gifted Scots writer. Better-known as J.M. Barrie, the author was born in Kirriemuir, Angus, and his home — 9 Brechin Road — now houses the Barrie Museum.

This year sees the centenary of *Peter Pan*, which was first staged at the Duke of York's Theatre, London, on December 27th, 1904. As well as the eponymous hero, it featured the now famous characters of Nana, Tinkerbell, the flying fairies, Captain Hook, pirates Smee and Starkey and the crocodile with the eight-day clock inside him.

Despite his writing fame much about James Barrie is mysterious. How did this naturally rather melancholy man come to write a children's classic? The answer is as complicated as the man himself. Barrie wrote *Peter Pan* in memory of all the people and places he loved best, so when the curtain rose on its first performance all these happy memories were drawn together. From that moment, the play has been a winner and a lucky one in which to act, according to theatrical superstition.

Who was the real Peter Pan? The answer is a very complex one. Barrie himself said

> It is as if, long after writing "Peter Pan", its true meaning came to me ... "

Part of Peter is the lonely child, miserable about being small for his age, that was Barrie himself. Another part of the character was Barrie's brother David who died aged 13. Most of all though, Peter was a mixture of five little boys — George,

David, Peter, Michael and Nicholas Llewellyn-Davies. Later Barrie became their guardian when their parents died young. He loved these children dearly, having none himself. Barrie longed to keep them "little boys" for ever, so *Peter Pan* was a fulfilment of that wish.

Who was Wendy? She was based on the angelic little daughter of Barrie's friend. Margaret Henley died tragically at the age of six, but the writer made her immortal. She had always called Barrie "my friendly", but because she lisped it sounded like "Wendy". Margaret loved to wear a little cloak, so the character of Wendy wore one too.

The motherliness of Wendy, however, came from the childhood of Barrie's own mother. As an eight year old she had to scrub, mend and bake for her little brother when their mother died. In this way Wendy became mother to the Lost Boys in the play.

The little house which the Lost Boys built for Wendy in Never Never Land was based on a shabby wash house! This was at Lillybank in the Tenements at Kirriemuir in Scotland, where Barrie grew up in poverty.

James Matthew Barrie, the Scottish writer who created the magical "Peter Pan". The play has enthralled children for a century.

Barrie included the pirates in memory of his school chums, who played buccaneers together in a garden at Moat Brae by the River Nith. One of the boldest was a friend of his at Dumfries Academy, Stuart Gordon, whose nickname was Daredevil Dick!

Arthur and Sylvia Llewellyn-Davies, the parents of the five little boys Barrie adored, became the inspiration for Mr. and Mrs. Darling. They were warm and loving parents, but tragically, both died young in real life.

(continued overleaf)

◁ *A scene from the 1904 production starring Nina Boucicault (Peter), Hilda Trevelyan (Wendy) and Gerald du Maurier (Captain Hook).*

life as he first introduced his master to the Davies boys during "walkies" in Kensington Gardens.

Barrie would tell his tales to the eager nursery audience of the five little boys at bedtime and one involved Peter Pan, the little boy so fearful of growing up that he ran away to live with the fairies in Kensington Gardens. Barrie told them:

By rubbing the five of you violently together, as savages with two sticks to produce a flame, I made the spark of you that is Peter Pan.

A Century of Peter Pan

continued

Knowing Barrie's love for all their children they made him their guardian on their deaths, a responsibility the now wealthy writer gladly accepted.

Who was the dog Nana? Arthur Lupino, from the famous stage family, took the part of this lovable dog on the stage in 1904, but in fact Nana was inspired by Barrie's own huge St. Bernard dog called Porthos! Porthos played an important part in Barrie's

Barrie and his actress wife, Mary Ansell, had no children of their own and eventually divorced following her infidelity. This parting hurt him and led to that strong melancholy of his later years.

There is a darker side to *Peter Pan* also, as in Peter's line: "It will be an awfully big adventure," quoted by Barrie's friend, Charles Frohman, the play's first producer — as he plunged to his death aboard the *Lusitania* in 1915. Some of the classic actresses

The very first production of "Peter Pan" was staged 100 years ago at The Duke of York's Theatre. This picture appears in the book "London Theatres" by Mike Kilburn, published by New Holland.

who have played Peter have captured his eerie, unearthly quality — a 19th-century Pan! They include Madge Titheradge, Gladys Cooper, Anna Neagle, Sarah Churchill, Julia and Margaret Lockwood and Nina Boucicault, the first Peter, all of whom became stars of their age.

The first Mr. Darling was actually played by Sir Gerald du Maurier, the uncle of the five Davies boys, so it was very much a family affair.

Three of the boys later died tragic deaths, yet there is still a spellbinding quality about this play. In April 1929, J.M. Barrie gave the copyright of *Peter Pan* to Great Ormond Street Hospital for Children. In 1988 Lord Callaghan's proposals enabled the Hospital to continue to receive royalties after the copyright ended in 1987. Curiously, Barrie left instructions that the amounts it received should not be disclosed. Yet another aspect of *Peter Pan* would remain a mystery to the end!

BEL BAILEY

The Redpoll

(Acanthis flammea)

by ROBIN RECKITT

This lively little finch is fairly common in this country, but often goes unnoticed due to its habit of feeding in the high tree tops; its small size and shape and sprightly movements could be mistaken for a blue tit. However, redpolls are more gregarious than the latter species and are usually seen in quite large flocks, sometimes in company with siskins, especially in alders along river-banks and in birch woods, their preferred habitat. In appearance they look rather like a linnet, but are much smaller in size with a distinctive scarlet forehead and black bib and have a fast bounding flight accompanied by a continuous twittering sound, also heard whilst feeding on tree seeds and buds. Like most bird species, the numbers breeding depend on the food supply.

Redpolls are a resident species but are also common all over Scandinavia, and when seed crops have failed there we get a big influx of birds from that area in autumn and winter. Unlike other species that return to their original nesting sites to breed, redpolls will stay here in the spring if the food supply is plentiful. In fact the Scandinavian race is slightly different, called mealy redpolls, being a bit larger in size and greyer (almost white sometimes) with a white rump instead of buff and of special interest to the ornithologist.

The nest is placed in a bush, bramble, hedge or tree at varying heights from the ground, made up of small sticks and moss, grass, wool and hair with a lining of feathers. Four to six deep bluish green eggs, speckled brown, are laid in May with sometimes a second brood later on. Small colonies of redpolls quite frequently nest close together.

There are also two further sub-species of redpoll apart from the mealy version with slight variations of plumage, again only of interest to the ornithologist or dedicated bird-watcher — they are, the lesser redpoll and the Arctic redpoll which hails from Greenland, Iceland, Jan Mayen and Spitsbergen. The female is similar to the male but has no pink on the breast. This is not a threatened species.

Colin's Christmas Tree

One Christmas in the late 1930s young Colin Way was delighted when his grandfather arrived at the door of the family bungalow in Kennington, Oxford, carrying a Christmas tree. Although the tree was not a traditional fir tree but a young Scots Pine, it served the purpose admirably when decorated with tinsel and a selection of colourful baubles.

In previous years his mother had always been the one to decorate the tree, with Colin having the honour of placing the star on top. This year however Colin asked if he could do it himself so was duly given the tinsel and baubles which he delicately arranged in a manner which he thought showed the tree off to its best effect. When the task was completed he gazed at it with pride as his parents and grandfather praised him for the wonderful job he had done. Colin went to bed happily that night, drifting off to sleep and dreaming of Santa and the presents he might receive on Christmas Day in a couple of days' time.

When Christmas Eve finally came Colin could hardly contain his excitement as he hung up his stocking on the mantelpiece in the living room. Suddenly, he started to wonder how Santa would know which chimney to come down. The scullery, back room and his parents' bedroom also had chimneys and he hadn't hung any stockings there. His father, Harry, soon put his mind at rest by reminding him that Santa had been there the previous year and already knew which chimney to use. This explanation satisfied Colin, and Harry was glad that the magic of Santa Claus had survived for at least one more year.

That Christmas was a jolly one as usual and when it was finally over Colin planted the small Scots Pine

tree in the garden, in full view of the rear window so he could watch it grow. It seemed to like the soil and became sturdy and tall during the war years when Colin would watch the trains go by at the end of the garden, loaded up with British troops on their way to fight in Europe. As they waved and whistled he wished he was old enough to join them, not realising that the focus of the soldiers' attention was usually two young ladies who lived next door. They would stand at the end of their garden blowing kisses to the troops and waving them merrily on their way.

By now, Colin's tree was visible over the garden fence and he was pleased when his neighbours said how pretty it looked.

By the time Colin was a young man his tree had grown several feet tall and he was sad to leave it behind when his parents sold the house in 1949 and moved out of the village.

Over the next 50 years the cottage changed ownership only three times before I moved there with my wife and family. We were captivated the moment we saw it and placed our offer on Easter Sunday 1998, presenting the owner with an Easter egg to clinch the deal in a memorable way.

The Christmas tree had by now reached over 50 feet tall, three times as high as the bungalow and completely overshadowing both our own garden and those of our neighbours. Despite having it professionally pruned and thinned it was all too apparent that as the years went by the tree would become even taller, requiring more expensive maintenance and becoming increasingly dangerous.

All that remains of the tree today is a stump — affectionately known as "Colin's seat".

Nevertheless the tree was a magnificent specimen and on some evenings, with the sun at a certain angle, its bark would turn bright red, as if on fire. It was also home to countless birds and some squirrels in addition to serving as a sturdy pole for washing lines, catherine-wheel fireworks and climbing clematis plants.

Unfortunately the tree was situated too close to the house so, having learnt about its history, it was with great reluctance that, last year, we decided to have it cut down. We thought the tree deserved a dignified and compassionate end so hired a reputable company of local tree specialists. They carefully dismantled each individual branch and within hours there was nothing left but a stump. On counting the rings we discovered that the tree was 68 years old, dating it back to 1935 and confirming its origins as Colin's Christmas tree all those years ago. The stump now serves as a sturdy seat, being in a prime spot of the garden which is exposed to the sun from dawn until dusk. We affectionately refer to it as "Colin's seat".

Sadly, Colin died in the 1980s while still in his fifties but he is still remembered by elderly local residents who watched his tree grow taller with each passing year. As for the two young ladies next door, Eve continued to live in the house until she passed away last year at the age of 90. Kath married and moved away, but later returned to live out her years with her sister and became a great-grandmother before also sadly passing away in September this year, aged 86.

By coincidence, about four years ago my own teenage daughter planted a tiny six-inch-high pine tree at the end of our garden. She had found it laying trodden on whilst holidaying in the countryside so decided it needed rescuing. It now stands over three feet tall. We were unaware of the history of Colin's tree at that time, so the discovery was very touching and it is gratifying to see that the fascination of youngsters with nature is timeless. Maybe the new pine tree will ensure that this Christmas story will be remembered for many more years to come. JOHN MCGHEE

Happy birthday ... to Evergreen !

It seems like only yesterday that we were announcing the "birth" of *Evergreen*. In fact, with the appearance of this issue, we have now completed 20 years of publication! Having reached such a landmark, we would like to thank each and every one of our loyal readers and hope that you will all continue to enjoy Britain's "Little Green Quarterly" for many years to come. We particularly appreciate your kind comments, a few of which are reproduced here.

Your magazine is avidly read by all my family. Thank you for the inspiration and enlightenment, colour, comedy and all. — BRIAN WEBB, NORTHAM, WESTERN AUSTRALIA.

The arrival of *Evergreen* brings a cooling English breeze into a world of hatred, terrorism, lies and deceit. Long may it flourish. — LINDSEY LITTLE, GREAT WHYTE, RAMSEY, HUNTINGDONSHIRE.

Thanks to you all for helping me to remember that I did grow up in a Britain that was tidy, had a kindly and considerate population and you could be patriotic without being accused of being "racist". — ALAN WARD, ENFIELD, MIDDLESEX.

For details of how to arrange a postal subscription, please turn to page 146. Alternatively you may telephone our order line on 01242-515156.

L.G. HIPPERSON

THEN & NOW

A series of photographs showing the changing face of Britain

Normanton

Until 1764 Normanton church in Rutland stood in the centre of a village. It was in that year that local landowner Sir Gilbert Heathcote cleared the settlement to create a park and moved the occupants to nearby Empingham. The church, dedicated to St. Matthew, with a semi-circular portico and tower, was largely rebuilt in 1826 to a design by Thomas Cundy and stood isolated in Normanton Park for many years (see the photograph, above).

In 1970 permission was given to flood the surrounding valley, and during the next few years it was swept clean of trees, hedges, cottages, farms and other rural remnants. However a great voluntary effort was mounted to save the church which would have been below the waterline.

As a result the floor of the building was raised by almost 10 feet and a causeway built to provide access. So, when flooding finally took place in 1977, creating England's largest man-made reservoir, this unique and historical church was saved as a memorial to the past. Now one of Rutland's most famous landmarks, it dominates the water's edge and houses a museum showing the history of the reservoir and surrounding area. The museum is open to the public between April and October.

Two tiny hamlets and the foundations of the original Normanton village now lie below Empingham Reservoir — known as Rutland Water — which covers 3,100 acres (about five per cent of the county) and holds 27,000 million gallons of water. It has a 25-mile circular track around its perimeter for cycling and walking. There is also a nature reserve and many bird-watching hides. On the water, sailing, windsurfing and canoeing can be enjoyed and a 45-minute pleasure cruise can be taken around the reservoir. It has the reputation of being one of the finest trout-fishing areas in Europe.

In 1974, as part of the controversial local government reorganization, Rutland, whose residents pride themselves on living in England's smallest county (motto: *Multum in parvo*, "Much from little"), was joined to Leicestershire, despite vigorous protests. Happily, in 1995, amidst much celebration, they regained their independence.

HENRY SPENCER

Field & Fireside

Rectory Rambles

When I heard my mother scream, I rushed into the kitchen.

"Don't come any closer, Angela," she said. "I'm going to gradually close the door."

I stopped suddenly as I saw the reason why. Standing facing my mother in the open doorway, as if about to enter, was a large, drooling Friesian cow.

"Go and tell your father to ring Fred Brown and let him know that his animals have escaped again."

I rushed as I was bidden but there was no need to pass on the message. My father was already on the telephone speaking irately, presumably to Farmer Brown, whilst watching from his study window a line of cows meandering up the drive.

A few minutes later Mr. Brown, whose farm was only across the road from our rectory, sauntered over,

The sprawling vicarage at Gorsley in Gloucestershire. As a girl, Angela, the author of the article, enjoyed rolling down the bank with her cocker spaniel, Banjo.

unperturbed, and gathered up his errant herd. Going out to meet him, my father had some very strong words to say, but Farmer Brown just laughed them off.

"They'm curious old girls, rector." he said. "They be always looking for adventure."

This was just one of the amusing anecdotes that I can remember from a childhood spent in Gloucestershire in the Forties and Fifties.

My father's parishes were all in the depths of the countryside and we lived in huge, draughty rectories, surrounded by vast, unkempt gardens. Upleadon, his first parish, had a mission church. I used to call it the "tin church" as it was made of corrugated iron and in the summer attracted swarms of bees. My few memories of this time include my godmother, Verena, nearly falling down a dangerously uncovered well, the heavy snow of 1947 and the subsequent floods through which we rode to Gloucester on the back of a lorry.

Our next move was to Gorsley, and the rectory opposite Farmer Brown's. I was a child of the outdoors and spent many hours rambling about the huge, wild garden. The house backed onto some woods that stretched as far as Newent, and every spring the gypsies would come to pick the daffodils that grew there in abundance to sell at the local markets.

My constant companion was a spaniel called Banjo. He was a rogue, and an expert at catching rabbits. My

Field and Fireside

(continued)

A family photograph taken during the early Fifties. Angela's older brother, Michael, also became a clergyman.

father would set traps because we loved rabbit stew, and Banjo would find them, steal the rabbits, eat his fill and leave the remains on the back doorstep.

We also kept chickens, and sometimes hungry foxes came out of the woods to steal them. Often the chickens would fly into the trees to escape and the next morning we would find them marooned in the branches. One hot summer night a bat flew into my bedroom. My father tried and failed to hit it with his slipper, so the rest of the night I slept elsewhere. Next morning it had gone.

The highlight of the year was the annual church fête, held in our gar-

den. I would wander about watching all the stalls being set up and later I'd spend my few pennies on sticky sweets or playing hoop-la.

The most popular money-raising event of every fête was "bowling for a pig". Skittles were set up at one end of a long wooden runway and people took turns to roll a heavy ball along it to try and knock them down. Behind the skittles was a barrier of straw bales and the balls were returned along a cleverly constructed downhill channel.

The prize for the winner was a pig, and the smelly, grunting animal would be in a pen nearby. I was amazed at why anyone would want

The old rectory at Shipton Oliffe, Gloucestershire, as it looks today.

▷ Angela, with her cousin Mary beside her, watches Mum and Dad riding a tricycle during a summer fête.

to win a pig, and in my innocence didn't realise that they would probably send it straight to market!

Later in the year we would join the potato pickers in a neighbouring field rented from the diocese by a church-warden. It was fun helping to gather up the potatoes and my father received several sacks as part of his stipend.

When I was about 13 we left Gorsley and moved to a parish in the Cotswolds. My father suffered greatly with recurrent bronchitis and the doctor advised him that the clear air

(continued overleaf)

Field and Fireside

(continued)

would be beneficial. The village was called Shipton Oliffe and it was here that we found ourselves living in the largest rectory yet. It had six bedrooms, huge attics, damp, green cellars, two staircases and an enormous bathroom. It was reached by a long drive and the garden stretched down to a stream crossed by a narrow bridge.

It was idyllic in the summer but in the winter the snow piled up on the inside of the windows, and the roof leaked, especially in my bedroom, causing me to lie awake listening to the rainwater as it dripped into a bucket. Most of the time we huddled around the warm Rayburn in the kitchen, and far from being beneficial

this cold house nearly killed my father. After three years we moved to a town parish.

Last year I took a trip down memory lane and revisited some of these old haunts, peering like a peeping Tom at the now privately owned, well-maintained and obviously valuable properties that had once been my home.

I wondered what the present affluent occupiers would say if they'd had to walk downstairs under an umbrella, or clear out a cellar full of frogs.

Perhaps they would have worn the same thunderous expression as my father when, seeing innumerable cow-pats all over the lawn, he was forced to listen to the non-church-going Farmer Brown say: "Course I be a Chris-chen. Look at all that lovely manure my girls have left 'ee. 'Twill do wonders for yer rhubarb!"

ANGELA BRADLEY

Room of Memories

A scented room, a treasured spot,
A book of memories
Where every sweet forget-me-not
Is pressed within its leaves.
It's here I love to sit awhile
And muse on days I miss,
I see a long-forgotten smile,
I feel a tender kiss,
The joys I knew, the tears I shed,
The laughter and the pain
In this old book are all re-read,
I laugh and weep again.
A touch of silk, a fragrant breeze,
A portrait on the wall —

But what a rush of memories
They kindle and recall.
O happy room I love so well
Nor e'er would lose the key,
No mortal tongue can ever tell
What you have meant to me.

J.M.JONES

Now where did I see that in
Evergreen?

Find out with the new up-to-date Evergreen Index
covering the magazine's first 20 years of publication.

It is hard to believe but *Evergreen* is now 20 years old, which means that since it was first published in Spring 1985 there have been 80 issues of Britain's "little green quarterly". Each article, poem and photograph featured in the magazine possesses a timeless quality and everlasting appeal so it's no wonder that readers are constantly seeking out back numbers in order to sample a second dose of the *Evergreen* tonic.

To help readers in their search for those favourite *Evergreen* gems from the past, a new index has been compiled. This 68-page alphabetical listing is easy to use and pinpoints the year, issue and relevant page number for every article, poem and picture which has appeared in the magazine over the last 20 years. In addition, there is a special, self-contained "Search for a Song" section and highlighted panels provide a comprehensive list of articles featured in such popular series as "Cinemagic", "Playing the Halls", "The Literary Pilgrim", "Almanac", "Rural Rides" and many more.

An indispensable addition to the bookshelves
of every Evergreen *reader.*

PRICE: £4.50 (inc. UK post). Overseas surface mail (airmail in brackets)
£5 (£6); or US $9 ($11); Can $12 ($15); Aus $13 ($16); NZ $15 ($19).

 **PO Box 52, Cheltenham,
Glos., GL50 1YQ.**

Telephone orders: **01242-515156** *(All major cards accepted)*

Winter snow and bare trees add a fairytale quality to the old Church of St. Peter at Preston, near Brighton, in Sussex.

The Evergreen Prayer

The leaves have gone, the trees are bare,
And birds begin their plaintive song.
No flowers now where once so fair,
The days are short and nights are long.

In the wild this time brings need,
All creatures haste to find their food,
The dark cold earth they do not heed,
Its dormant state will make for good.

Snow falls and covers all the ground,
The scene takes on an eerie face,
Breathtaking beauty all around,
Pure and with a virgin grace.

Lord Jesus makes the winter bright,
Dispelling all the cold and fear,
The babe born on that starlit night,
You bring to us such joy and cheer.

BRENDA SHARP

Well-loved programmes from the world of wireless

A midst the sound and bustle of cars, buses and taxis circling Eros in Piccadilly Circus, plus a train, an aircraft and a ship's whistle, could be heard a broad Cockney flower-seller called Mrs. Baker saying "Here you lady (lidey!) dear, luvly sweet violets". Also blended in was Eric Coates's *Knightsbridge March*, and a newsboy shouting: "In town tonight, in town tonight" then, in a slightly higher voice: "In town tonight" before a very loud voice roared: "Stop!"

In Town Tonight

The silence was then broken by a BBC announcer: "Once more we stop the mighty roar of London's traffic and, from the great crowds, we bring you some of the interesting people who have come by land, sea and air to be *In Town Tonight!*" When the programme was later televised, a film was shown of traffic in Piccadilly Circus being halted. As a little boy, Bruce Forsyth wondered what the

poor drivers did for the next 30 minutes while they waited patiently in their vehicles. He was not alone!

The programme was transmitted on the Home Service every Saturday from 7.30 until 8pm at the end of which a stentorian voice of authority shouted: "Carry on, London!" when the traffic on the film started to move again. When the venue moved briefly to Manchester then they stopped the traffic flowing into Albert Square.

In Town Tonight began on 18th November, 1933, when an extraordinary galaxy of stars took part. Included were film star Bette Davis; composers George Posford and Annette Mills (later of *Muffin the Mule* fame); cartoonist Robert Ripley; actress Gwyneth Lloyd; and singers Austen Croom-Johnson, Paul England and Tessa Deane.

The biggest coup, however, was the Stonemason's Dance Band. Led,

This typically busy scene in Oxford Street, London, during the mid-Thirties, shows 40 buses, 12 taxis and various other vehicles. As a small boy, Bruce Forsyth used to listen in with his parents at the start of In Town Tonight *and, like thousands of other children, believed that all the traffic actually ceased moving for 30 minutes immediately the stentorian command of "Stop!" was given.*

theoretically, by Britain's first disc jockey, Christopher Stone, it included band leaders Henry Hall, Jack Hylton, Ray Noble, Lew Stone, Jack Jackson, Harry Roy, Howard Jacobs, Carroll Gibbons, Ambrose and Geraldo. How about that for an all-star turn?

There were usually eight slots in the programme but contrary to the public image they were edited and meticulously rehearsed in advance. Lionel Gamlin was the first studio interviewer while Michael Standing went out and talked live to people in the street during the cleverly-named item "Standing on the Corner". Later celebrity presenters included Roy Rich, Gilbert Harding, John Ellison, Alan Keith, and Brian Johnston who was also responsible for another live section called "Let's Go Somewhere".

Starting in 1949, Johnston sought out unusual and sometimes dangerous activities and was so successful in his quests that in February 1955 he was given his own show under the same name: "Brian Johnston is out and about with his live microphone, looking for laughter, excitement, and anything else he can find". He always located it too, with a familiar chuckle en route. One Christmas he crammed himself into an Oxford pillar box but kept it secret until on air so that students did not come and post anything apart from letters and parcels!

Programme number 500 was broadcast on 26th November, 1949, with Annette Mills putting in another appearance. By now the eight separate parts were linked by short snatches of music, taken mainly from

(continued)

Robert Farnon's *Journey Into Melody, A Star is Born, Portrait of a Flirt* or *Jumping Bean*. Fittingly, also included on this occasion was the composer of the signature tune.

Eric Coates was often described as the "Uncrowned King of British Light Music" but this was due in no small measure to the remarkable set of circumstances which saw the *Knightsbridge March* first recorded. The other two movements of his new *London Suite* (*Covent Garden* and *Westminster*) were already safely in the can when someone played a wrong note in the final movement. Take two was going well until the wax master broke. With musicians paid strictly by the hour and the seconds now ticking up to one o'clock, Coates had to plead with everyone to give it just one more try … and what a magnificent job they made of it!

Amazingly, only shortly before *In Town Tonight* went out for the first time, the producers suddenly realised they had forgotten to select any introductory music. An urgent call was therefore made to Chappell's record library in Bond Street requesting anything they could find with the name "London", from which *Knightsbridge* was hurriedly selected.

In his Baker Street flat, not far from Broadcasting House, Eric Coates was in his dark room developing pictures when his wife Phyllis called out: "They're playing something of yours on the radio but I don't know what it is." Coates emerged briefly, listened and replied: "No, neither do I!" then disappeared back into the gloom. He was soon disturbed again, however, because when the programme ended there was a flood of phone calls asking for details of the tune, many of which were diverted straight to the composer's home.

More than 20,000 others wrote in asking the same question and Eric Coates and the *Knightsbridge March* became overnight celebrities. Even 70 years later, the trombones blasting out the oompahs in this great melody, combined with vivid memories of the disembodied voice shouting "Stop!" still send tingles down the spine.

Radio was very much king during the Thirties and the upsurge of independent broadcasting from Europe, especially Radio Luxembourg (see *The Ovaltineys* in *Evergreen*, Spring 2001) brought a new popular music dimension. The BBC was rather staid by comparison and started haemorrhaging listeners but then someone realised that early Saturday evenings on the Continent did not include any English-speaking programmes.

The die was cast and although there was considerable live domestic opposition from both cinemas and

(continued overleaf)

CELEBRITIES
WHO WERE
"In Town Tonight"

◁ *Also a wax-modeller, John Tussaud was the great-grandson of the original Madame Tussaud.*

▷ *Gypsy Petulengro was a well-known fortune-teller and showman who travelled extensively during the Thirties.*

Churchman Cigarettes issued
this set of 50 cards in 1938
by which time
the programme had
become a national institution.

◁ *Toni and his monkey, Yento, were a one-man band once tipped half-a-crown at Epsom races by Queen Mary.*

▷ *Prince Monolulu was a colourful Abyssinian racing tipster, famous for shouting "Ivegottanorse!".*

△ *Mrs. Emma Baker was the voice of the broad Cockney flower-seller in Piccadilly Circus heard during the opening of* In Town Tonight.

△ *The Pearly King, Queen and Prince of Blackfriars broadcast to the British Empire and also appeared at the radio and television show, Radiolympia.*

(continued)

dance halls, *In Town Tonight* was an immediate success. Famous celebrities were matched carefully against unknowns with a story to tell and whole families gathered around the wireless to listen. It was hard not to be moved by the lady who lost four of her eight sons in the First World War, with a husband and daughter also permanently incapacitated by bomb damage to their home.

The sixth floor studios at Broad-casting House were adequate for small numbers of people but St. George's Hall next door was often used for larger gatherings. It was also used for finding the railway porter with the loudest voice and a man playing the posthorn at full volume!

Among the unusual interviewees was a Sudanese princess from the Sahara Desert. She spoke no English but was rehearsed word-perfect by her sponsor. Fortunately, the presenter asked the questions in the right order, otherwise it would have turned into a comedy routine.

The public always listened attentively and could be relied upon to respond when a need arose. An out-

Danny Kaye (centre) once secretly connived with producer Peter Duncan (right) to upset the schedules with his typical zany antics live on air. They are seen here in company with another famous guest, Sir Ralph Richardson.

of-work fire-eater was immediately offered an extended tour of Africa, and a door-to-door London salesman who, at different times, had rescued 26 children from the Regent's Park Canal, was promptly offered jobs both as a commissionaire and a caretaker!

The programme attracted more than 300 letters a week and when a move was made to take it off there was a public outcry which brought about its rapid reinstatement. Mr. and Mrs. Joe Public and all their little publicans — for this was a true family affair — thoroughly enjoyed the format. Producer, Peter Duncan, had many contacts and was always able to conjure up something unusual.

In 1938 a set of 50 cigarette cards was issued among whom were a lady chimney sweep, a Petticoat Lane trader, a one-man band, a rat-catcher, a flower-seller, and a master magician. Celebrities included the outrageously colourful racing tipster Prince Monolulu, the fortune-teller Gypsy Petulengro, singer Parry Jones and author Algernon Blackwood.

A regular and popular guest was Danny Kaye who often popped in from the London Palladium down the road. On one occasion he secretly and mischievously connived with the producer to upset the show by pretending to extract the electricity sockets and distracting the other guests

Brian Johnston was one of the earliest and most successful outside broadcasters who spent a lifetime working for the BBC in various guises.

while on air. At the end he pinched the scripts from the continuity announcers and did the closing credits all by himself.

Programme number 714 took to the air on 3rd April, 1954, and made history as the first radio show to appear simultaneously on television: quite a challenge even for experienced presenter, John Ellison. New features were tried, including "Number One Dressing Room", "Talk of the Town", and "Just Touched Down". One of the latter was the American singer of the mid-Fifties hit record, "Davy Crockett, King of the Wild Frontier", but he either died of stage fright or was suffering from jet lag because halfway through the third

(continued)

verse he suddenly sang: "Hum, hum, hum, forgotten the words"!

However, with the advent of ITV in 1955 the televised version soon ran into trouble. Saturday night viewing had been quickly transformed by the new independent companies and their slick and fast-moving schedules proved far too much for the more sedate BBC who quietly dropped out of the race. Set against *Wyatt Earp* and the *64,000 Question*, there was no contest.

Nevertheless, the programme continued on the radio for another five years and broadcast number 1,000 was celebrated on 6th August, 1960. However the *Knightsbridge March* and "Carry on London!" were heard for the final time only five weeks later on 17th September. A brief revival on 26th July, 1975, marked the closure of the BBC Light Entertainment Dept. at the Aeolian Hall.

Stars of yesteryear were always worth listening to, which is where they part company from their more modern counterparts, and the reason why *In Town Tonight* lasted so long.

PETER WORSLEY

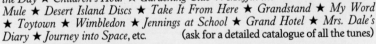

Castles
&
COTTAGES

A charming, rose-fringed cottage at Millington in the East Riding of Yorkshire.

Belsay Castle in Northumberland was built as a tower house in the 14th century. A manor house was added to the original building in the 17th century.

Recalling some of Variety's favourite turns

The art of ventriloquism was at its height during the days of variety when even a second-rate performer could get away with his lips moving slightly. One of the more polished acts, however, was given by a lady who first tried her luck while still only nine years old.

When her teacher asked for volunteers for the Christmas concert, Winifred Fox immediately put up her hand. Asked to explain her act she replied "Talking dolls". Already well-trained because her father was a professional magician called Professor de Lyle, her performance was so good that she was asked to give it to each of the other classes in turn!

A Yorkshire girl, Winifred was born in Sheffield on 18th September, 1903, and was surrounded by theatri-

Wynne de Lyle the lady "vent"

cal tricks of the trade. The year 1916 saw both father and daughter giving succour to wounded soldiers with Winnie's two dolls renamed Sister Susie and Tommy Atkins. On Christmas Day she performed in no fewer than six different hospitals.

At the age of 14 she followed her father's footsteps into the local Sheffield Co-operative Society (CWS) and soon puzzled her boss by calling his name without him realising where the voice was coming from. She was later caught out, however, when he heard laughter and silently tiptoed into a room where he discovered Wynne entertaining her fellow workers using a brush as a dummy. She was extremely embarrassed and quickly returned to work.

It was not long, however, before

How it all began. Young Winifred Fox at school in Sheffield with Punch and Judy, two of her father's stage props.

This is how she ended up after being persuaded to leave Sheffield Co-op and tread the boards as a professional.

her natural talent was recognised and she received several requests to emulate her father on stage. After leaving the Co-op she toured the country and while performing in Leyland, Lancashire, she set up a prank with the help of her elderly landlady's grand-daughter whose policeman fiancé was in the habit of taking a break on his night shift. Dressed as two burglars they waited for him to enter the house in the dark before Wynne put on her best masculine voice talking about "swag" and not waking up the neighbours. He immediately put on the light and brought

his truncheon down on the dummy!

On another occasion her luggage was searched on a routine customs check at Dover. The diligent officer was somewhat taken aback, however, when what he initially thought was a dead body suddenly started talking to him out of the suitcase.

Summer seasons were spent in the east coast resorts of Norfolk, Suffolk and Lincolnshire but all too soon Wynne found herself entertaining troops again, this time in the Second World War. "Jimmie", her dummy, was dressed up as an RAF officer complete with pilot's wings while

▷ This photograph is dated 1944 and signed "Yours ventriloquily, Wynne de Lyle". She is dressed as a member of the WAAF and her dummy, Jimmie, as an RAF pilot officer. As in the First World War, they entertained troops whenever possible but now Jimmie was able to descend onto the stage by parachute.

◁ A happy post-war picture of Wynne with her husband Herbert Weller at the piano and a rather posh-looking Jimmie, the dummy. Sadly, following some reckless driving by a group of American servicemen returning to base, she died in a car accident at Dunstable in 1953. She was only 49 years old.

Wynne herself appeared in a WAAF uniform. Her excellent act was made even more memorable as Jimmie parachuted down onto the stage.

Wynne de Lyle as a young lady.

In 1946 she married a widower called Herbert Weller and they enjoyed seven years of happy life together before she was killed in a tragic road accident near Dunstable in Bedfordshire. It was caused by a reckless overtaking manoeuvre by some American servicemen returning to base. Her husband, who was driving, survived the impact, as did her mother who was travelling in the back but both never got over the shock of losing their loved one.

A lady vent is unusual. Wynne de Lyle was one of that rare breed and a very good one too.

EDMUND WHITEHOUSE & MAURICE ROBSON

Continuing…"A Year to Remember"

Listen to the popular songs from your special year

Young or old, everybody has at least one special year which seems to stand out in the landscape of life. Generally, it's their birth year — even though no-one can remember it! — but it could also be some other important event. Now, with this new series — eventually stretching from the Twenties to the Fifties — you can spend an intriguing hour listening to the memorable music and discovering the special events of the year concerned. Each CD highlights the popular songs which first emerged in that year, and each inlay card details the main events that occurred — the headline news, sporting successes, famous births, etc.

Produced by *Evergreen's* own studio engineers from original recordings made at the time, these 60-minute *"Year to Remember"* CDs make ideal low-cost gifts for your parents, spouse, friends or relatives. The series already includes the late Twenties (1926-29), the Thirties (1930-39) and now continues into the Forties. 1940-44 are now available, to be followed later by 1945-49 and the early Fifties, 1950-54. And remember — these CDs are exclusive to the readers of *This England* and *Evergreen*, for they are not available in any shop. So order now and start your journey down memory lane …

One hour of the most memorable music from that special year!

CD PRICES:
only £8.95 each (inc. UK post).
Overseas surface mail (airmail in brackets)
£10 (£11); or US $18 ($20); Can $24 ($27);
Aus $27 ($30); NZ $31 ($34).

SPECIAL OFFER: Buy 3 CDs and get the
fourth one FREE!

Evergreen, PO Box 52, Cheltenham, Glos. GL50 1YQ.
Telephone orders: 01242-515156   All major cards accepted

A YEAR TO REMEMBER 1920

One million are unemployed, of whom a third are servicemen from the Great War who had hoped to return to a country fit for heroes. Conscription is abolished in the wake of the Treaty of Versailles, while the League of Nations holds its first meeting.

Europe is in turmoil as thousands of displaced nationals return to their homes. France occupies the Ruhr; Italy is paralysed by strikes; Russia attacks Poland and Finland; Turkey massacres 10,000 Armenians and when Constantinople is occupied by the Allies, Mustafa Kemal sets up a rival government in Ankara; the Slav town of Fiume declares war on Italy; and Estonia declares independence.

In Germany a royalist coup is put down in Berlin; the socialists capture the industrial town of Essen and the Nazi Party is formed. In the Middle East, Arabs attack the British in Palestine while France invades Syria.

Events of the Year

●**Home Affairs:** Sinn Fein wins 73 seats in Ireland but refuses to turn up at Westminster. Ulster Unionists threaten to secede if Dublin is given authority over all Ireland. A terrorist war erupts with street fighting in Londonderry put down by the British Army. Both Sinn Fein and Ulster Unionists riot in Belfast before Prime Minister, Lloyd George, accepts partition as inevitable. Northern and Southern Ireland are given separate parliaments and open war occurs between Irish nationalists and a volunteer British army unit nicknamed the "Black and Tans".

British miners go on strike for an extra two shillings a week. This government message to the nation has been posted over the top of London theatre bills.

●One million British miners strike for nearly three weeks in support of a pay claim for an extra two shillings a week.

●**Social history:** Baden Powell convenes a second international Boy Scout convention.

●100 women undergraduates are admitted to Oxford University.

●The Medical Research Council is established.

●At 11am on 11th November, the new Cenotaph in Whitehall is unveiled by King George V, followed by interment of the Unknown Warrior at Westminster Abbey.

●**Foreign Affairs:** Russian Bolsheviks are defeated in Poland but capture Odessa and Sebastopol, ending the White Russian domination of Crimea .

●In Germany, factions of the left and right clash in several towns. A peaceful march in Berlin ends in bloodshed after demonstrators trying to enter the Reichstag are met by armed police who fire into the fleeing crowd. Adolf Hitler takes control of the German Workers' Party and denounces Jews and Marxists.

Prohibition becomes law in America with illicit liquor being destroyed.

●Tomas Masaryk becomes President of Czechoslovakia and Admiral de Nagybanya of the new state of Hungary. Both are anti-communist.

●**The world at large:** The American Post Office rules that children may not be sent by parcel post!

●In Hollywood, silent film comedian "Fatty" Arbuckle is charged with murder but declared innocent. His career grinds to a halt, however.

●In Mexico the president, General Carranza, is assassinated by a fellow General. Pancho Villa finally lays down his arms under an amnesty which ends years of mercenary conflict in the north of the country.

Charlie Chaplin and Jackie Coogan star in the silent film "The Kid".

●Warren Harding becomes the new Republican President of the United States; American women win the vote; the Recording Company of America (RCA) takes to the international airwaves for the first time; and prohibition becomes law.

●**Films:** Charlie Chaplin appears with Jackie Coogan in *The Kid*, while heart-throb film-star Mary Pickford marries equally famous Douglas Fairbanks.

●**Popular Songs:** *After You've Gone; Alice Blue Gown; I'll Be With You in Apple Blossom Time; I'm Forever Blowing Bubbles; The World is Waiting for the Sunrise* and Al Jolson's *Swanee*.

●**Music:** Vaughan Williams's atmospheric *The Lark Ascending*.

●**Sport:** Britain wins several gold medals at the Antwerp Olympics. West Bromwich Albion win the Football League and Aston Villa the FA Cup, beating Huddersfield Town

Mary Pickford & Douglas Fairbanks

1-0. Middlesex win the county cricket championship and "Big Bill" Tilden is the first American tennis singles champion at Wimbledon with Suzanne Lenglen (France) winning the ladies' event. *Troytown* wins the Grand National, and *Spion Kop* the Derby. Golfer George Duncan triumphs in the British Open.

●**Births:** Karol Wojtyla (Pope John Paul II) and Isaac Asimov, American science-fiction writer.

●**Obituaries:** Lord Fisher, leader of Britain's Navy during the Great War; Empress Eugenie of France, former wife of Napoleon III; Robert Peary, the first explorer to reach the North Pole; composer Max Bruch; and King Alexander I of Greece.

BERNARD COLLINS

Our Christian Heritage

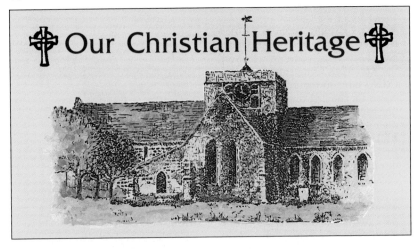

igh up in the Purbeck hills of Dorset lies the chapel of St. Aldhelm. The only way to reach it is along a stony track leading from the village of Worth Matravers. The track is just over a mile long, but if you're walking it in high heels and wedding finery it can feel a good way further!

The sight of the chapel, on its windswept cliff overlooking the English Channel, is a welcome one after such a walk. The views out to sea and back inland are far-reaching and emphasise the chapel's isolation.

St. Aldhelm, who died in 709 AD, was the first Bishop of Sherborne. The chapel bearing his name appears to date from around the 12th century, but no records survive to confirm this. There is evidence, however, of the site being a Christian enclosure

The Chapel in the Hills

long before that: earth mounds encircling the chapel suggest that Christians worshipped here well before the Norman Conquest.

The chapel itself is small and squat — just 35 feet square. Thick stone buttresses support the outer walls, and unusually the corners, rather than the walls of the building, are aligned with the points of the compass. The chapel's entrance is low and narrow and set toward the end of the north-west wall.

Inside, it takes a while to become accustomed to the darkness, but it is possible to make out the font beside the door and the rows of pews ranged down two sides. These seat just 40 people, and meet at the modest altar in the east corner which is illuminated from behind by the chapel's only window.

Ramblers rest against the ancient stones of St. Aldhelm's Chapel in Dorset, high on a hilltop overlooking the sea.

KEN AYRES

The vaulted roof and light-coloured stone pillars maximise the space but do little to dispel the extreme dimness. There is also no organ installed here: the chapel's predisposition to damp means that musical instruments have to be taken in for each service.

Clearly, St. Aldhelm's was built to serve the spiritual needs of the community, but it is curious that it is situated so far from any nearby habitation. Some people believe, therefore, that it might have served a secondary purpose, helping to defend the area by covering the "blind" side of Corfe Castle a few miles further inland. Its

Our Christian Heritage

(continued)

position on the headland is certainly ideal for spotting potential trouble approaching from the sea.

Whatever the truth, the chapel was used regularly for services of worship until the 17th century. By this time, however, it was in a state of disrepair, and in the mid-1800s the roof had collapsed completely. Shortly afterwards a programme of renovation was undertaken by a local landowner and the chapel reopened in 1874.

There are other stories about St. Aldhelm's. One concerns the central pillar which was found to contain hairpins when the repairs were being carried out. It was thought that the pillar had been used like a wishing well, with pins dropped in through a hole.

There is also speculation over the roof. The large cross which currently adorns it dates back to the time of the repairs, but it is believed that it was preceded by a beacon cresset. If so, this might support the idea of St. Aldhelm's being a lookout post, or the light could simply have been used to warn sailors off the rocks.

The chapel has been used fairly regularly ever since reopening and today is popular with both visitors and worshippers. So it is worth making the journey along that bumpy track — although perhaps not in high heels!

NINA CURLE

As the saying goes ...

A "Dead Ringer"

When a person is described as a "dead ringer" for somebody else, it means they look exactly like them. The phrase refers to the practice of unscrupulous racehorse owners who, having a fast horse and a slow horse which were identical in appearance, ran the slow horse in races until the betting odds became attractive. They then backed the horse at these long odds, but ran the "ringer" (the faster horse) in the race. "Ringer" is Australian slang for the quickest sheep shearer in a group. "Dead", in this case, means exact or absolute.

The 2005 Evergreen Pocket Diary
Your handy, day-to-day companion and friend ...

This smart *Evergreen* pocket diary is perfect for keeping up-to-date with appointments, birthdays and holidays. With its distinctive green cover, gilt foil lettering, and measuring 6" x 3¼", it fits neatly into a pocket or handbag and makes the ideal Christmas stocking-filler.

Contains a comprehensive diary section (two weeks to view with Sunday start), a detailed calendar and maps covering motorways and rail networks. A special section compiled by the *Evergreen* editorial team includes birthday and anniver-

Actual size
6" x 3¼"

sary information, words of wit and wisdom, lists of Great Britain's traditional counties and principal towns, plus collections of autograph verses, humorous epitaphs and weather lore. Only available direct from *Evergreen* — not for sale in any shops.

·FROM·THE·EDITOR'S·CHAIR·

When it landed on the mat amongst all the bills and junk mail, I hadn't a clue what it was. The envelope was illustrated with what looked like a row of those old 45rpm records you used to get — "singles" I think they were called — and each one had a different colour in the centre and a drawing of a strange symbol. I knew right away that it wasn't a music catalogue, because beneath the row of discs were the words "Important Information From HM Government". Curious as to why HM Government should write to me, I tore it open immediately and found, to my great surprise, a white booklet, decorated with the same circular objects, entitled *Preparing for Emergencies: What You Need to Know.*

I don't know if anybody else has received the booklet, although I suppose they must have. The government would hardly single me out for special protection! But in case any readers have missed out, I thought I ought to describe it and pass on some of the important information.

Those small discs also appear inside the booklet, but instead of coloured symbols in the centre there are photographs of some of the officials involved in preparing for emergencies. It's a strange way of showing their faces, giving the impression that they are looking through car tyres, but that's a minor quibble: it's the instructions that are important.

First of all, if you do "find yourself in the middle of an emergency" you must remain calm and, if possible, think before acting. The authors give details of a three-figure number you should ring (999) and urge you to help yourself before assisting others. Oh yes … and you should also carry out a check to see if you are injured. It's obviously important that you don't forget to do this.

As a general rule, in the face of an emergency, people are advised to go inside a building, stay inside, and tune in to their local radio station. To help you remember this procedure, something called the "National Steering Committee on Warning and Informing the Public" has produced, after much discussion, a catchy phrase: *"Go in. Stay in. Tune in"*. It is quite helpful — I think, at long last, it is now fixed in my head — although I do keep getting it mixed up with that hippy mantra of the so-called Swinging Sixties: "Turn on. Tune in. Drop out". I think that was something to do with escaping from the world by watching television.

Having told people to go inside a building, the booklet does warn them they should not do this if the building is on fire. Similarly, if you are in a house where there is a fire, you should get out and call the fire brigade. There are helpful guidelines for other possible scenarios, again advising courses of action that most ordinary people would never think of. If, for instance, a bomb goes off in your building, you should look for the safest way out; and anyone at the scene of a chemical attack needs to move away from the source of the danger. I assume you should do this quickly. It doesn't say.

I don't want to cause panic, but if a large number of these booklets have been produced it must have cost thousands of pounds so there must be some sort of threat. I suppose we are fortunate in our government. A less scrupulous one might, for a variety of reasons, doctor the intelligence and exaggerate the danger. And fortunately, it isn't all doom and gloom. There is a reassuring section informing us how well prepared the emergency services and security forces are, and a description of the state-of-the-art surveillance systems at points of entry into the country. It's certainly comforting to know that we aren't admitting illegal immigrants or bogus asylum seekers who then disappear without trace so there is no way of telling if they are terrorists or not.

At the end of the booklet we are informed that it is also available in Bengali, Chinese, Arabic, Urdu, Punjabi, Somali, Welsh, Gujurati, French, Greek, Kurdish, Farsi, Turkish, Vietnamese and Hindi. I did not realise there were so many people living in this country who do not speak English!

Let us hope that it never happens, and I don't believe it will, but it conjures up a dreadfully chaotic scene at the telephone exchange when all those 999 calls start coming in …

First Telephonist: "I'm afraid I can't understand you. Does anybody here speak Urdu?"

Second Telephonist: "Help! I've someone on the line speaking Swahili."

Third Telephonist: "I can speak Punjabi, but my caller is Arabic."

Fourth Telephonist: "My caller is Chinese. I speak Urdu."

Fifth Telephonist: "I speak Hindi and Gujurati, but my caller is Kurdish."

Sixth Telephonist: "Does anybody here speak Welsh?"

Have a merry Christmas and a happy, peaceful — and safe — New Year!

S.G.

STATE MEMORIES

SIR: "Music Makers" (Spring 2004) mentioned the State at Kilburn. My father, a famous theatrical agent of the time, sadly died in a car crash in 1934 when I was a baby. My mother was a dancer and had been a Tiller Girl before moving on to her own act. She was invited to the opening night at the State — such a magnificent place and Europe's greatest theatre. I have the opening night programme, with all the history and planning of this luxurious building and details of the famous people who appeared that night.

As I grew up I went to it as a cinema hundreds of times in all its splendour and saw it camouflaged during the war. Although I live in Hertfordshire now, I have revisited it, but it is heartbreaking. I know it is a Grade II listed building, but its marbled floors and classical renaissance decoration have been spoilt. Just looking at the building, now used for bingo, is so sad. — R. TUCKER, ABBOTS LANGLEY, HERTFORDSHIRE.

DESTINATION ETERNITY

SIR: Back in the 1960s, I was a Methodist Theological Student. One dark Sunday evening in November I was returning, by train, to Manchester after conducting services in one of the local churches. The journey had been terribly slow, with constant stops and starts. As we came to a standstill yet again, I looked out of the carriage window and my attention was caught by a flashing neon sign. It read "Where will you spend eternity?" Whatever the answer to that question I hoped it would not be on a train en route to Manchester Piccadilly! — REVD. CANON A.J. KERSWILL, LINCOLN.

RATION SURPRISES

SIR: I am a volunteer at the Great Torrington Heritage Museum in Devon and the most popular exhibition of recent years is our 1940s house. In this we have a display of a week's rations of the period. This causes amazement, particularly amongst children when they see a plate with three small rashers of streaky bacon, one sausage and one egg. "Is that what you had for breakfast?" we are asked. The surprise comes when we tell them it represents breakfast for a week!

Two things always cause comment from our more mature visitors. One is the weekly sugar ration of eight ounces. This invariably brings the remark: "That's more sugar for one person than we use for our whole family for a month today." And the other is from older visitors who lived through those times and could not remember that bread was not rationed until after the war and that rationing continued until 1953. — A.A. REEVE, DOLTON, WINKLEIGH, DEVON.

Despite rationing, I think that the wartime diet was far healthier than what many people eat today. — Ed.

LADYBIRDS & TRUMPTON

SIR: On reading the last two editions of *Evergreen*, childhood memories were stirred, firstly by the excellent piece on Dr. L. Du Garde Peach ("Byways", Summer 2004) and the fascinating journey back to Trumptonshire ("TV Memories", Autumn 2004).

However, what was not mentioned was the role played by L. Du Garde Peach in the story of the Ladybird Books, for it was Dr. Peach who provided much of the stirring and informative text to the history titles of that series. I still have my original Ladybirds which tell the story of Cromwell, Nelson, Charles II — all written and illustrated in the most exciting style, and ideal for younger children.

The puppet-people of Trumptonshire, although "simple" entertainment, never-

The Editor invites letters from readers for this feature but regrets he is unable to reply or acknowledge them, except by occasional comment in these columns. Letters must contain the writer's full name and address (not necessarily for publication) and the Editor reserves the right to abbreviate where necessary. Please address letters to: "Clippings", Evergreen, PO Box 52, Cheltenham, Glos., GL50 1YQ.

theless conveyed a gentle sense of the old England — especially with the character of Lord Belborough! Whenever I see these old, poignant, now almost forgotten books and films, I cannot help thinking that today's generation of children have missed something truly special and important. — STUART MILLSON, EAST MALLING, KENT.

I'm sure that many readers will echo your thoughts, sir. — Ed.

More 'CLIPPINGS' over the page...

(continued)

MYSTERY CHURCH

SIR: I enclose a picture (see below) which was taken some years ago and escaped being labelled. It shows a shaped sheet of lead from a church spire which records the years when it was repaired, the work done, the cost and the names of the architect, the church wardens and the plumber, together with their ages. I hope that the church has preserved this interesting relic, in spite of its hole, and that perhaps one of your readers might know of its location. — B.R. BURROWS, SHIPLEY, YORKSHIRE.

*Our eagle-eyed readers are bound to come up with the answer! — Ed.

NAVY STARS

SIR: My first beau was on board *HMS Ganges*. Early in the war they were allowed to wear the ship's name on their hats. Going out with him in London, to the cinema in Leicester Square, to see *In Which We Serve*, we were fêted by people and received chocolates and cigarettes. I recall being with him in Folkestone, interviewed by the local press, when he stated: "If we'd had as much ammunition as we had kisses from the local ladies, we'd have seen them all off before!" — GWYNETH FLOOD, FOLKESTONE, KENT.

ZEPPELIN RAID

SIR: Recently, my mother came across a letter written by her 17-year-old sister to her brother during the First World War. The letter contains a rather moving account of a German Zeppelin raid over London, part of which reads:

> You wanted to know about the Zeppelin raid, well it was very exciting ... I had just started my supper when Muriel heard the guns, it was simply deafening, we immediately went upstairs and woke the others. Muriel was in hysterics and Mrs. Mulligan was deathly white. The three old maids came in from

◁ *A piece of lead from a church roof containing details of repair work carried out in 1802-03. But does anyone know the location of the church? See letter this page.*

next door and brought all their valuables, papers, money, jewellery etc., and they were frightened, their teeth were chattering and their knees playing a tune. Luckily I did not feel nervous, though of course it wasn't very nice to hear everyone saying their prayers and waiting for the end to come, of course I must admit some of the people were too nervous altogether, they gave way completely. Well I saw the Zeppelin, and the guns were firing at it from Lambeth Bridge... and you should have seen the shells bursting around the horrible thing. The special constables were all calling out and the police whistles going all the time, the despatch riders were coming up to the bridge very frequently. I loved to hear the sentries shouting "Halt! Who goes there?" all the time the guns were firing with great rapidity... the scene was never to be forgotten. The Zeppelin passed practically all over London, they even saw it in South Kensington, and when it was lit up by the searchlights it looked like a huge silver cigar and was indeed very pretty. In the City the damage was fearful and Waterloo Station was greatly damaged, 106 casualties altogether. A motor bus outside the station was blown up, and all they could find of the driver was his leggings in the next street. Isn't it all very horrible?

— BRIAN THURSTON, OAKLANDS, WELWYN, HERTFORDSHIRE.

What an incredible account. It must have been absolutely terrifying. — Ed.

(continued overleaf)

(continued)

PUT AND TAKE

SIR: I not only recall playing Put and Take ("Clippings", Autumn 2004) in the 1940s, but still have the actual brass spinning top, with which we played the game. This was given to me by my grandma. As I was born in Wakefield and the correspondent gives a Pudsey address, could the game have been popular mainly or exclusively in Yorkshire? — WILBERT DAVIES, HOLT, NORFOLK.

SIR: I remember the small brass hexagon bar from the mid-Twenties when it was used for gambling! If I recall correctly I also remember my mother and a friend examining it and saying that the Government had banned the further manufacture of same as it was encouraging some men to lose their pay packets even before they got home on a Friday night. — MRS. R.K. CAREY, TAVISTOCK, DEVON.

SIR: We spent many happy winter nights around the table playing Put and Take as well as Table Skittles, Bob Cue — on the floor with the carpet rolled back — dominoes and cards. My father ruled that the winners always got an orange and the losers had to sit on a balloon and burst it! Then we all ended up around the big open fire making toast on a toasting fork. We didn't need computer games, we made our own fun, they were really happy days. — ROSEMARY O'CONNOR, OREWA, NEW ZEALAND.

SIR: We also played Put and Take with buttons, but the game didn't seem to last very long. My father went to a fancy dress as a Put and Take, but he didn't get a prize as the judges had never heard of it! — FLORENCE McROBERT, SKIPTON, GARGRAVE, YORKSHIRE.

Many thanks to everyone who has written in with their recollections. — Ed.

NARKOVER CHARITY

SIR: With regard to Brian Simpson's letter about the Narkover School badge ("Clippings", Autumn 2004), Will Hay was the leading figure in the Narkover College charity. This supported soup kitchens etc., providing sustenance to the down and outs in the Thirties. The charity was funded by the fees for membership of Narkover College and the lapel badge you illustrate was worn by College members. It was a good system for getting further money out of the curious! — ALAN WHITE, MINSTER IN THANET, KENT.

SIR: I have a 10-inch gramophone record of Ronald Frankau, accompanied by Monte Crick, performing *Don't do the Dirty on a Fellow Narkovian* and *A Lecture from the Moral Adviser*. Upon the label is printed "The profits from this record are being paid to Narkover College in aid of St. Peter's Kitchens." During the Thirties the Kitchens gave some succour to the poor of London and Mr. Simpson's Narkover badge was that of a supporters' group. — MICHAEL JAMES-AP-JOHN, LOUGHTON, BUCKINGHAMSHIRE.

Did You Name The Stars?
— pictured on page 41

Hayley Mills

Juliet Mills

Sir John Mills

It was John Mills supporting his two daughters, Juliet (left, born 1941) and Hayley (born 1946). He was knighted in 1977 and his wife was Mary Hayley Bell. Hayley's dramatic debut was in *Tiger Bay* (1959), playing a child witness to a murder investigated by her father, a police superintendent. Her later films included *Pollyanna, Whistle Down the Wind* and *The Parent Trap* when she took the parts of identical twins who successfully plotted to bring their long-separated parents back together.

MIDDLESEX MARCH

SIR: *Sweet Lass of Richmond Hill* ("Clippings", Autumn 2004) is also the Regimental March of the Middlesex Yeomanry (Duke of Cambridge Hussars), but with this difference. The WRAC march has a refrain in the middle:

Early one morning, just as the sun was shining, I heard a maiden singing in the valley below.

The Middlesex Yeomanry Regiment was raised in Uxbridge in 1797. The band was subject to defence cuts in 1968, but continues to this day as the Middlesex Yeomanry Association Military Band and is based in Hampton, Middlesex. The 47th (Middlesex Yeomanry) Signal Squadron is still in Uxbridge. — MAJOR (RTD.) R.L. MILLER, ASHFORD, MIDDLESEX.

RANDOLPH'S HOUSEKEEPER

SIR: The letters about Randolph Sutton ("Clippings", Autumn 2003, Spring 2004) were of great interest to me. My late mother, Marion Margaret Thomas, who came from South Wales, was housekeeper to Randolph and his sister. I still have two letters that Randolph's sister sent to my mother, who was in hospital at the time, asking her to come back to them when she was better as they were missing her. My mother was always singing *On Mother Kelly's Doorstep* (one of Randolph's songs) and a lot of Welsh songs too. — MRS. CECILIA BORRINGTON, WIN-SHILL, BURTON-ON-TRENT, STAFFORDSHIRE.

More 'CLIPPINGS' over the page...

(continued)

BETTY'S CLEANER

SIR In 1949 I became Betty Box's ("Cinemagic", Autumn 2004) cleaner when she had a flat at Sheffield Terrace, Kensington. Every day she left a note saying what had to be done. I never met her, but I always received my money and a "thank you" note for looking after her home so well. At Easter and Christmas there was always a present and extra money. I stopped cleaning for her when I had my third baby.

Later I worked for Bebe Daniels and Ben Lyon and the film star Greta Gynt. I cleaned and cooked for her guests who included Gregory Peck. He asked for Dover sole and commended me on a lovely meal. When he went back to America he left a silk shirt behind and she gave it to me. — BETTY HOWARD, WEEDON, NORTHAMPTONSHIRE.

What fascinating memories. — Ed.

MEMORIES OF PC 49

SIR: I was sorry to discover that Brian Reece (PC 49) had such a short life ("On the Air", Autumn 2004). In 1953 he found the time to come out to Malaya during the emergency, with a couple of supporting artists, to entertain the troops. The conditions were very primitive with only bowls for washing and makeshift changing facilities and no sound equipment. Despite this they put on very enjoyable shows.

This was a conflict that cost so many lives of civilians, police and our troops, but it was hardly known about back in the UK or reported on by the media. The artists who came out to our isolated units did not do it for publicity or personal gain, just a desire to entertain. One was Hy Hazell and the party, the other was Brian Reece. I am sure that any of the troops who experienced these shows will always be very grateful — N.M. BEARD, GLENMORE PARK, NSW, AUSTRALIA.

◁ *The actress Greta Gynt (1916-2000). An "Evergreen" reader used to cook and clean for her as well as other stars. See letter this page.*

The delights of afternoon tea at Sidmouth in Devon. Two "Evergreen" readers have opened a traditional English tea-shop in Australia. See "Tea-time Treats".

ADINA TOVY

TEA-TIME TREATS

SIR: One of our customers has recently donated some back issues of your magazine to our English tea-shop and we happened upon your story of "Molly Lolly" in New South Wales, Australia ("Clippings", Summer 2001). We would also like to share our story.

We emigrated to Australia in March 2003 to set up Pommes Teashop in Wynnum, Brisbane. Our shop is as traditional and authentic as is possible and we have a large Welsh dresser, brass wall lights, linen and lace tablecloths, and many items of antique china and glass, as well as an extensive range of books on England, Ireland, Wales and Scotland.

We make all our products on the premises and our customers enjoy such treats as Eccles cakes, Cornish pasties, Scotch eggs, cottage pie, Bakewell tarts, lemon meringue pies, bread and butter pudding and traditional victoria sponge cakes. We also pride ourselves on our indulgent high teas which are served on three-tier cake stands in the proper manner. As well as these goodies, we also make ploughman's lunches, filled Yorkshire puddings and our own, hand-

---

More 'Clippings' overleaf

'Clippings'   *(continued)*

made scones and clotted cream (following the traditional Cornish recipe).

We definitely celebrate St George's Day and the local radio station came and interviewed our customers on this day — it took them over two hours as our customers had a lot to say! — ASHLEY & NICOLA BYWATER, WYNNUM, QUEENSLAND, AUSTRALIA.

Sounds delicious! — Ed.

Evergreen Overseas

*E*vergreen now has local offices in the Pacific and North America which can handle enquiries and orders from readers.

Although most goods will continue to be despatched from the UK, a small stock is held in these offices (detailed below) for immediate despatch. There is a small surcharge for this service. Please enquire with local offices for details.

AUS: Evergreen, PO Box 14,
Sassafras, Vic 3787.
Tel (03) 9755 1834
Fax (03) 9755 3455
e-mail: australia@thisengland.co.uk

NZ: Evergreen, PO Box 9373,
Newmarket, Auckland
Tel (09) 585 1280
Fax (09) 585 1281
e-mail: newzealand@thisengland.co.uk

USA: Evergreen, PO Box 6435,
Santa Barbara, CA 93160, USA
Tel (1-800) 607 4489
(10am-6pm) *(California time)*
Fax (805) 964 1702
e-mail: usa@thisengland.co.uk

CAN: Evergreen, PO Box 91037,
West Vancouver, British Columbia
V7V 3N3
Tel (604) 913 1484 (24hrs)
Fax (604) 913 1485
e-mail: canada@thisengland.co.uk

SHELLS, JACK & HUGH

SIR: The Shell Gardens (Summer 2004) was a unique place and so many visitors enjoyed its beauty. To be described as "past its sell-by-date, just a load of old shells stuck on a wall" was a complete travesty and the local reporter should feel ashamed of him/herself. I can't find words to describe the monstrosity now in its place, but of course money and greed are the key words in today's society. For me and my family the Shell Gardens is sadly missed.

The amusing Initial Confusion item ("Scrapbook", Autumn 2004) brought back memories. I lived in Canada in the late 1950s/early 1960s and I watched a television programme from America — *The Jack Paar Show.* Jack was ably assisted by Hugh Downs and they caused lots of laughs. On one show Jack read the letter about the WC; he could hardly get his words out and the audience were in stitches.

However, the next night a very sombre Jack opened his show. Apparently various church groups in the USA had contacted the producers to voice their disgust at the letter and all had demanded that Jack should make an abject apology. He did this and then, to everyone's amazement, walked away, leaving Hugh to take over. He didn't return, despite the support he received. I often wonder what has happened to Jack and Hugh. — VERA SENNECK, REDHILL, BOURNEMOUTH, HAMPSHIRE.

In fact, Jack Paar did return to his show a month later, but left for good in 1962. His television programme was hugely popular and he interviewed many famous people ranging from Judy Garland to Fidel Castro! He died in January this year, aged 85. — Ed.

St. Patrick's Isle on the Isle of Man is said to be haunted by a mysterious black dog, the Moddey Dhoo. See letter below.

HAUNTED ISLE

SIR: I enclose a photograph (see above) of St. Patrick's Isle on the west coast of the Isle of Man which is haunted by the Moddey Dhoo ("Almanac", Summer 2004). Excavations show that the island was inhabited since 500 BC. Until the end of the 18th century it was only joined by a causeway to Peel. — MISS COSTAIN, COLBY, ISLE OF MAN.

PICKET LINE

SIR: I was very young during the General Strike ("First-Class Service", "Clippings", Summer 2004), but I used to hear my late dear father talk of this dreadful time, when men were striking for a better wage, which then was under £2 a week.

My father, who owned a jam factory on Tyneside, had already been paying his staff a better wage and for this the pickets allowed lorries going into his factory a free passage through. — CICELY MERRILEES, KEITH, BANFFSHIRE.

THROAT EXERCISE

SIR: "Wonderful Whistlers" ("Clippings", Summer 2002) reminded me of my early teens when I was having voice training lessons. The teacher asked if I ever whistled? I replied "Yes, but my Mother and Granny do not like it". My teacher then explained it was the finest exercise for your throat. Imagine my delight in telling them at home that I had to exercise my throat by whistling! — BETTY MARPLES, NORTH WALSHAM, NORFOLK.

ALL OUR YESTERDAYS

".......but for Heaven's sake, don't say I told you!"

I n 1941, with the men being called up to go into the fighting forces, my mother, Mary Scadden, was required to do her part and help the war effort. She had been doing various jobs in Weymouth after leaving school, but as soon as she became 18 the expected letter arrived to say that she was to report to Redbridge in Southampton to undertake 16 weeks of training to become a welder. Welding had always been a man's job, and it was only through sheer necessity (a lack of welder's mates) that women were allowed to learn such skilled work.

Mary worked in a factory unit learning her trade alongside Naval personnel. She did become very homesick but was able to travel back to Weymouth every weekend, so life wasn't too terrible. Whilst at Redbridge she was trained to weld

My mother was a welder's mate!

sitting down, and when the "slag" was knocked off the new weld it would often fall off the bench and land on her bare skin between her trousers and her shoes. When this was pulled off it took the top few layers of skin with it and was excruciatingly painful.

After her initial training she moved to Vosper's in Portsmouth, once again working in a factory unit welding equipment for the Services. Here she met many RAF aircrews who had been badly burned and she was initially horrified at their disfigured faces.

It was during this period that she received her first "flash". When a welder puts the welding rod down to the metal an electric arc is drawn which is extremely bright. If the mask is not put in front of the eyes immediately the light intensity burns the reti-

na and a "flash" occurs. She had been a welder for a while by this time, and as she had not had any problems with flashes she assumed she would never get one! She was wrong, and consequently had the horror of not being able to see. It felt as though her eyes were filled with hot grit and the only relief was to put a cold flannel over them. No one took any notice, as it was considered to be an occupational hazard that would make her remember to use her mask correctly in the future! After about 24 hours her eyes were as good as new and she got back to work.

Mary worked with many women from all over the country. They were

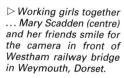

▷ *Working girls together ... Mary Scadden (centre) and her friends smile for the camera in front of Westham railway bridge in Weymouth, Dorset.*

(continued)

lodged in houses or bungalows and the couples who owned the houses were excellent chaperones, making sure that the girls were in on time and did not keep any "bad company". As they all worked shifts, it was possible to see friends during the day. Her father Leonard was in the Merchant Navy, stationed in Portsmouth, so it was a great treat to get a visit from him and to go out for a meal.

In 1942 Mary decided the time was right to move back home and she requested a transfer to the Dockyard at Portland. It was a dangerous area as there were many air attacks on the base, and in March 1941 the school in Fortuneswell, just above the Dockyard, had been bombed and sustained substantial damage.

Her request was approved and she gratefully returned home to her own bed and her mother's home cooking. Life was not easy for the people who lived in Weymouth, and on 2nd April, 1942, 20 died and 56 were injured when Nazi dive-bombers swept across Weymouth Bay; one bomb destroyed the *Dorset Daily Echo's* office in the centre of town.

On arrival at the Dockyard, Mary was assigned as a welder's mate to Leonard Thomas, skilled tradesman. They worked, as Mary had before, at a bench maintaining the vessels. She was also required to visit the tugs that were tied up alongside the quay. She was frightened as she walked up the gangplank to the deck of the tug, but remembered her father's advice: if she held on, she couldn't fall into the churning sea below. On the mornings that she worked on the tug, the sight of it riding the waves made her stomach queasy and she was never able to eat her sandwiches when she got to the mess.

Often celebrities arrived at the Dockyard's canteen to entertain the workforce. Mary remembered the day that Joan Regan sang, enabling them to forget, just for a while, that they were in the middle of an awful war and their husbands, fathers and brothers were away fighting.

At the end of each day, as they left the Naval Base to catch their buses,

---

Sweet Memories

Pineapple chunks, cherry lips,
Sherbet fountains, liquorice sticks,
Barley sugars, acid drops,
All within my favourite shop.

The counter was tall,
But I was small!
Sweet shop memories
I fondly recall.

DIANNE FELLOWES

The ornate clock, created for the Golden Jubilee of Queen Victoria in 1887, which stands on the Promenade at Weymouth in Dorset.   JAMES WARMAN

they had to pass the Dockyard police who searched workers at random to check that they were not taking any food or clothing off the boats. Mary was much too frightened to attempt to smuggle anything out, but it was done by some.

In 1945 Mary met Joseph Maddern who was in the Navy and whose ship had recently been torpedoed. He was stationed at Portland whilst his ship was being refitted and so stayed longer than he might have done. They were married in December 1945 and, in February 1946, Joe was

moved to Portsmouth. Mary "retired" from her welding job and moved with him. Her skills were not needed once the war was over.

For an 18-year-old the war years had been both exciting and frightening. Mary had met troops from many countries of the world and had watched the American troops leaving Castletown Dockyard preparing for the invasion of Normandy exactly 60 years ago. She didn't feel frightened for herself, but knew that her mother worried about her family every day. When their country called them, these young people answered the call. I wonder if we would manage to do the same if it happened in 2004?

JOSEPHINE BUTCHER

Two of the life-size dinosaurs — Iguanodon — which survived the fire at Crystal Palace in 1936 and continue to intrigue visitors to the site in south-east London.

GRANDMOTHER'S DRAGONS

My grandmother was a born story-teller and as a child I heard numerous tales of her young days. Like many other girls she had been in service, and one of her jobs was at Sydenham in south-east London. On her days off she would visit Paxton's glorious "conservatory", the Crystal Palace.

She filled my imagination with stories of the wondrous things she'd seen there including the magnificent firework displays and the "monsters and dragons" that stood on islands in the lake. Benjamin Waterhouse Hawkins, a noted sculptor, made them of brick and iron, covered with stucco, under the supervision of Professor Richard Owen, the eminent Victorian zoologist who coined the word "dinosaur" which is Greek for "powerful lizard". Besides the pterodactyl,

An old postcard of the Crystal Palace during its heyday. Some of the most memorable events to take place there were the spectacular annual firework displays witnessed by tens of thousands of spectators.

the iguanodon and the giant sloth, there were many others. They enchanted me and I treasured the souvenirs my grandmother gave me: postcards, a pencil case, and a picture showing a ferocious creature which looked like a crocodile.

I don't think her visits to the park were entirely educational. After her death, when I was sorting out her papers, I came across faded photographs of her, and other young ladies, in the company of soldiers who were billeted in the park before they were demobbed at the end of the First World War.

On the evening of 30th November, 1936, long before I was born, the Palace burned down. With that conflagration went my chance of ever seeing the dinosaurs — or so I thought. Little did I know, when I went to work in Croydon, and to live in Upper Norwood, that I would find my childhood wonders still there.

I thought that all that remained of the Crystal Palace was the name borne by a football club, so you can imagine my surprise when, exploring my new neighbourhood, I found the park and came across a collection of prehistoric monsters peering out of the shrubbery! They had been battered by the years, but were still lords of their domain.

My granny's "monsters" lived, not only as a testament to Victorian science but to the power a story can hold over a child's imagination. How pleased I was to have them back.

T.W. JENKINS

THE EVERGREEN BOOKSHOP

The following books
are offered to readers by mail order.
All prices include postage and packing (surface
post overseas). Airmail rates on request.

'THE WHIMSICAL WORLD OF COLIN CARR' — Now also in softback!

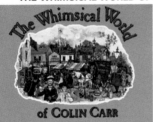

Village characters, eccentric entertainers, bustling market places ... the unique illustrations of Colin Carr have delighted readers of *This England* and *Evergreen* with the arrival of every issue. Sadly, Colin died in 2002 at the age of 73, but he left behind a treasure chest of colourful paintings, more than 100 of which are contained in this lavish book — an affectionate tribute which also includes a biography of the artist written by the Editor, a lifelong friend since their boyhood days in the Lincolnshire fishing port of Grimsby. The book (sized 11" x 8½"), which is not available in the shops, is already proving to be a best-seller, so please order now to avoid disappointment. See also page 79 in this issue. Price: *Softback:* **£14.95** plus £2 post & packing to UK addresses. Overseas surface mail (airmail in brackets): **£17.95** (£20) or US $32 ($36); Can $44 ($49); Aus $48 ($54); NZ $55 ($62). *Hardback:* **£20** plus £2 post and packing to UK addresses. Overseas surface mail (airmail in brackets): **£23** (£26) or US $41 ($47); Can $56 ($63); Aus $62 ($70); NZ $71 ($80).

NEW! — A TREASURY OF THIS ENGLAND

Ever since the first edition of our sister magazine *This England* was published in the spring of 1968, each quarterly magazine has been packed with fascinating articles, beautiful photographs, inspiring pieces of poetry and interesting letters from readers all over the world. Now, in this lavish new book, readers can rediscover and enjoy once more many of their favourites. Divided into seasonal sections, the *Treasury of This England* will take readers on a satisfying journey of nostalgia. Articles include "Rutland: Whatever Happened to England's Smallest County?", "Keats in the Lake District", "The Spring Folklore of England" and "The Man Who Invented Cat's-eyes", as well as colourful pictorial features such as "Royal Album" and "English Summer Album", and illustrated poems by G.K. Chesterton and Rudyard Kipling. Orders are already pouring in, so we look forward to making the *Treasury* an annual event. 144pp, hardback. Price: **£14.95** inc. post and packing to UK addresses. Overseas surface mail (airmail in brackets): **£17** (£22) or US $34 ($44); Can $45 ($58); Aus $46 ($59); NZ $53 ($68). See also page 43 in this issue.

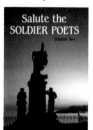

A fishing boat quietly and unobtrusively slipped out of Waterford harbour on the morning tide one fine day in May 1778. On board were two members of the Irish aristocracy — two ladies who were running away from home. They had waved a sad farewell to Kilkenny Castle and Woodstock, their respective Irish homes, where they had been most unhappy. Their destination was Milford Haven in South Wales.

In due course these two lifelong friends travelled to Llangollen in North Wales and decided to make their home in that delectable spot. High above the town and the River Dee they found a remote stone cottage. This was "Plas Newydd" — "the new place" — which over the years became famous as the home of the two Ladies of Llangollen: Lady Eleanor Butler and the Honourable Miss Sarah Ponsonby. They were to remain there until death claimed Lady Eleanor 50 years later at the age

The Ladies of Llangollen

of 90, and Miss Ponsonby, aged 76, two years after that.

Lady Eleanor was an enthusiastic and able gardener, and with the help of her friend she filled the borders of "Plas Newydd" with a colourful assortment of flowers including spring-flowering brooms, yellow laburnum, white lilies and a selection of roses that filled the air with perfume on a summer's evening. Cherry trees and poplars were planted at the back of the garden to give a touch of vertical artistry to this pleasant spot.

Miss Ponsonby drew and painted — she was also the housekeeper. The ladies read extensively, their library being full of rare books. Lady Eleanor kept a diary which gave an interesting picture of their rich, cultural and social life in the Vale of Llangollen.

The ladies were renowned for their hospitality, kindness, wit and huge circle of friends which included the aristocracy of Britain, great literary figures and men and women of fame.

Set in beautiful gardens, "Plas Newydd", the curious black-and-white home of the Ladies of Llangollen, is now a museum.

DAVID HUNTER

Amongst these were William Wordsworth, Sir Walter Scott, the Duke of Wellington, Thomas De Quincey and Edmund Burke, fresh from France at the beginning of the French Revolution. Another visitor, Count Jarnac, gave the ladies a vivid account of the storming of the Bastille — they were interested in all current events both at home and abroad. Wordsworth offered a sonnet as a gift, but after referring to the house as a "low-roofed cottage" he wasn't invited again!

Llangollen was one of the favourite stops for travellers making their way between London and Dublin, so everyone of note would pay a social call on the ladies. They had a passion for collecting old carved oak for

A view of Llangollen from the River Dee, with children exploring the rocks and looking for signs of life in the shallow waters.   ADINA TOVY

adorning their plain stone-built residence, and the custom was established that every visitor would bring along a gift of something special in old oak or a curio of note. The carved lions on the exterior were presented by the Duke of Wellington.

The people of Llangollen looked upon the ladies as eccentrics of the first order. In 1820 Charles Matthews, the actor, wrote this description:

> *... seated there is not one point to distinguish them from men — the dressing and powdering of the hair, their well-starched neck-clothes; the upper parts of their habits which they always wear even at a dinner party, made precisely like men's coats and the regular black beaver hats. They looked like two respectable superannuated old clergymen.*

Lady Eleanor died in 1829 and Miss Ponsonby in 1831; they are buried in the local churchyard. "Plas Newydd", the home of the ladies, is now a museum and visited by thousands of people each year. It is noted for its fine carved woodwork, but there is more to the house than that. The ladies have made their presence felt over the years and put their own stamp on the house and gardens. Even today, as you walk through the ornamental garden to the house, it is easy to imagine they are still there.

E. EMRYS JONES

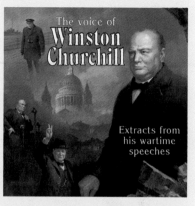

Footlights and Fancy

Toy theatres were a joy to make,
A simple cardboard box supplied our need,
We sketched our actors, painted all the scenes,
And turned out plays and pantomimes with speed.
The velvet curtains, pulled aside, revealed
A world of pure enchantment and delight,
Excitement mounted for the audience
So rivetted and spellbound at the sight.

Pretty coloured candles served as footlights,
Small and twisted from the Christmas tree,
Their scalloped holders clipped on to the stage,
To be extinguished later for safety.
But, oh, the thrill of lighting them again!
Seeing the glow, watching the shadows fall
On players we created, on the scenes
In elfin forest or in baron's hall.

Such were childhood pleasures in those days,
That this was one of many little treats,
For, in the interval, as curtains closed,
There were wheels of liquorice, bootlaces and eats,
Bought at Mrs. Butcher's tiny shop
Prize packets, bull's-eyes, tiger nuts,
A barley sugar stick, a lollipop.

There were spectacles made of gelatine,
Acid drops and Sharp's cream toffee slabs,
Scented cashews, all in pastel shades,
Lemonade crystals and sherbet dabs;
Oil lamps, from Gran's day, had disappeared,
Gas light came and went; the rage
Was for the clean, new, bright electric light,
But our delight, at our age, was the stage.

ROSEMARY YOUNG

A Calendar of Customs and Folklore

The English theatre has some wonderfully eccentric customs. The Baddeley Cake is a favourite of many actors that has endured for more than 200 years.

Robert Baddeley was the 18th-century actor who made quite sure he would always be remembered by his fellow thespians after his death. In his will, he bequeathed the interest from a £100 investment to provide a merry Twelfth Night party for whatever group of actors was currently playing at his beloved Drury Lane Theatre in London's West End.

His instructions included the baking of a huge fruitcake, which was to be cut and served in the Theatre's Green Room, where the cast relaxes after the evening performance. Punch and wine to toast his memory were also to be served. Baddeley's wishes have been ceremoniously observed since his death in November 1794.

Although the Baddeley Cake has entered the realms of theatrical folklore, comparatively little is known about Robert Baddeley's life and career. Believed to have been born on April 20th 1733, we know he was orphaned at an early age. In the years before he met actor-manager, Samuel Foote, he was employed as a pastrycook and had spent three years travelling the continent as valet to an aristocratic gentleman. It was during his young, impressionable years that he acquired a smattering of continental

A Twelfth Night Theatrical Tradition

languages and an awareness of foreign customs which were to serve him well later on in his acting career.

He became chef to Samuel Foote, from whom he acquired an interest in the theatre. Recognising Baddeley's talent for the stage, Foote gave him his big chance by offering him the part of Sir William Wealthy in his new comedy, *The Minor*, at the Haymarket Theatre on June 28th, 1760. This role was included in his debut at Drury Lane a few months later.

Although Baddeley played many characters in his first season, he realised he had a penchant for light comedy, often playing continental parts. He became a successful, established member of the Drury Lane company, playing numerous roles over the next 32 years. Occasionally, he made charity appearances at other theatres including Covent Garden, Bristol and Richmond.

Baddeley possessed sartorial elegance and enjoyed his reputation as a dandy. At the age of 30, he eloped with 18-year-old Sophia Snow, the daughter of Valentine Snow, sergeant-trumpeter to George II. Unfortunately, within a year or two, the marriage failed. Sophia was extraordinarily beautiful, but also extremely vain and reckless. She developed theatrical yearnings and Baddeley introduced her to the world of acting. She appeared on the Drury Lane stage and became an overnight success, excelling in musical productions.

Robert Baddeley, the 18th-century actor, who instigated a Twelfth Night celebration at London's Drury Lane Theatre.

As the Baddeley marriage became increasingly acrimonious, they each took lovers. On March 17th 1770, George Garrick, brother of David, the famous actor-manager, fought Baddeley in a bloodless duel over Sophia. An article reporting the duel appeared in *Town and Country Magazine* the following week and

'Almanac'

(continued)

The cast of the musical "Miss Saigon", which was staged at Drury Lane Theatre, drink a toast to Robert Baddeley.

was accompanied by an engraving depicting the incident. The Baddeleys never officially divorced, but were legally separated later. Thereafter, they often acted together on stage, although it was reported that they never addressed each other "except when the utterance was dramatic!" Sophia died on July 1st 1786, aged 46, in poverty.

Whilst on stage, during his evening performance as Moses Shadrack in Sheridan's *The School for Scandal* on November 19th 1794, Baddeley, then aged 61, suffered a stroke and died early next morning. He had played the character Moses over 200 times

since his original performance on May 8th 1777 and had made the part famous. His funeral was attended by leading London actors.

Although never rich, Baddeley was comfortably off. He left the bulk of his estate to his last partner, Mrs. Catherine Strickland, which, after her death, reverted to the Drury Lane Theatrical Fund of which he had been a founding committee member since 1774. Unfortunately, when Strickland died there was very little of the estate remaining. Baddeley left precise instructions in his will. As well as the Twelfth Night bequest, he desired that on the anniversary of his birthday, April 20th, the directors of the Theatrical Fund should reprint Baddeley's letter to the *General Advertiser* of April 24th 1790 "as various printed books and pamphlets have grossly misrepresented the disagreement between my late unhappy wife and myself". He wished by this means to let posterity know he had not merited the villainy imputed to him.

Although a good actor, Baddeley rarely played the great tragic parts which were fashionable at that time. He was skilled in portraying national characters such as Dr. Druid in *The Fashionable Lover* and Fluellen in *Henry V*. Although his Swiss and German parts were admirably characterised, his portrayal of aristocratic Frenchmen sometimes received criticism as can be discerned in part of the cutting verse written by a reviewer in *The Secret History of the Green Room*, a year after his death. However, bear in mind the bloody revolution that was going on in Paris at that time!

His skill in Frenchmen has procured his name
No scanty portion of theatric fame
Yet, though we own that Baddeley can trace
Their mean servility and pet grimace …

Many paintings of Sophia and Robert Baddeley remain. The distinguished theatrical painter — Zoffany — painted Baddeley as Moses in *The School for Scandal* which was exhibited at the Royal Academy in 1781 and is now part of Lady Lever's collection at Port Sunlight. In the Garrick Club there is a large canvas, also by Zoffany, of a scene from *The Clandestine Marriage* portraying both Baddeleys which was painted at George III's command as a result of the monarch's delight at seeing a performance at Drury Lane on October 12th 1769.

Other paintings, engravings, drawings and a few woodcuts of Sophia and Robert Baddeley are displayed in the Harvard Theatre Collection in Boston, Massachusetts, the British Museum and the Shakespeare Memorial Theatre.

One thing is certain — this forthcoming Twelfth Night, when the powdered, bewigged flunkies, dressed in 18th-century livery, bring the punch and giant Baddeley Cake into the Theatre Royal's Grand Salon, the assembled thespians will drink an affectionate toast to Robert Baddeley, honouring his wish to be remembered in the theatre he loved so much.

SYLVIA KENT

Country Crafts

Every country community in Britain once boasted a large number of specialised craftsmen and workers who were essential to the smooth running of the rural economy. This series, illustrated by John Edwards RP, RAS, looks at some traditional crafts and occupations — continuing with the seed fiddler.

B y the third quarter of the 19th century manual sowing for corn and similar crops was becoming unusual, with horse-drawn seed drills and dibbing machines taking over from men walking in line tossing out seed.

For sowing grass, however, hand broadcasting remained common. It was a skilled task, executed at a steady gait if there were not to be uneven coverage and bare strips. Skilled sowers were highly valued, with the best capable of covering half an acre a day and able to earn top money by hiring themselves out at piece rates.

For single-handed broadcasting the usual container in Scotland was the sowing sheet, worn like a sling and wound tightly around the arm in which it was cradled, while the English preferred a wicker basket. The method was to cast to one side (usually the right) over half a ridge, with the other half being covered on the way back. For double-handed sowing the operator would strap around his waist a large box, often called a seedlip, into which he would make alternating dips.

Then, late in the 19th century, there appeared a revolutionary invention — the sowing fiddle. It derived its name from a horizontal bow that, drawn with each stride, set a wheel revolving and discharged a smooth and even spray. In one easy motion the seed fiddler could cast an arc up to 30 feet wide. From half an acre a day the experienced hand could now comfortably expect to manage three or more acres an hour — true progress!

EDWARD CAMPION

A far cry from the mechanisation of today — this painting shows Stan Howes, of Bewdley in Worcestershire, sowing seed by using an instrument known as a seed fiddle.

Last Lines

Instead of our usual humorous epitaphs, we decided to bring you a selection of memorable final words delivered by famous people before they shuffled off this mortal coil.

Am I dying or is this my birthday?
LADY NANCY ASTOR

I should never have switched from scotch to martinis.
HUMPHREY BOGART

That was a great game of golf fellers.
BING CROSBY

I've never felt better.
DOUGLAS FAIRBANKS Snr.

Put out the light.
THEODORE ROOSEVELT

Go away. I'm all right.
H.G. WELLS

Recipe for Life

David Oyston from Gilstead in Yorkshire thought that these lines would appeal to *Evergreen* readers:

*Take a large amount of laughter
    and some teardrops mixed with
    sighs.
Add to this some sunshine,
    and the smile of merry eyes.
Collect two cups of morning dew,
    dilute it with some rain,
Stir it well with happiness,
    but season it with pain.
Pour this in a golden cup —
    buttered well with strife,
Wrap it up with problems,
And that, my friends, is life.*

Hoarder's Verse

We're all guilty of hoarding things at some stage in our lives, and what's to say it's a bad habit? Edward Needs from

Is it a bird, is it a plane? No, it's a hot air balloon in the shape of Bertie Bassett flying high above the city of Oxford. It just goes to show that you see "allsorts" in the sky!   DENIS KENNEDY

Newport, Monmouthshire, is a self-confessed hoarder and he wrote this poem chronicling the fact:

I'll put this away for the children,
It's a pity to throw it away.
I'll put it with some of the others,
It's sure to come in handy one day.

I'll find room in the attic; for this one
They don't make these things any
   more,
I'll wrap it in plenty of paper
And lie it down flat on the floor.

This should just about go through the
   trap-door,
With a shove and pull with a rope,
There's nowhere else we can put it,
So let's try once again and just hope.

I'll layer a few more of those
   "thingees",
And take a few cuttings of these,
I'd better sow some of those whatsits
And grow a few more little trees.

Now the attic and shed seams are
   bursting,
In the garden are more odds and
   ends,
But it seems that the children won't
   have them,
Instead they may well go to friends.

For half of the kids have departed,
To lands that they feel are more just,
In the meantime our odd bits and
   pieces
Will get thicker and thicker in dust.

Scrap Song

Many readers will remember the time when people were encouraged to donate their old pots and pans to the war effort.

(continued overleaf)

(continued)

Aluminium saucepans were used in the manufacture of planes and this was just one of several National Salvage Drives organised by the government. This amusing song was written at the time to remind housewives of the importance of recycling:

> My saucepans have all been
>   surrendered,
> The teapot is gone from the hob,
> The colander's leaving the cabbage
> For a very much different job.
> So now, when I hear on the wireless
> Of Hurricanes showing their mettle
> I see, in a vision before me,
> A Dornier chased by my kettle!

Feathered Friends

Although robins are seen throughout the year, they are traditionally associated

with Christmas. *Evergreen* reader, John Reid, from Broxburn in West Lothian, encountered one whilst out gardening and he was prompted to write this tribute:

R   ed breast to the fore and gleaming
O   blivious to the winter drear
B   eady-eyed and fearless-seeming
I   nto my heart you bring such cheer
N   ature's little champion

R   eassuring in the wannish sun
E   ach time I see you in my garden
D   eclaring another day begun
B   ird of courage are you bred
R   esplendent in your waistcoat red
E   mblem of the nation's love
A   s daylight fades and you adjourn
S   o little bird I make this plea
T   omorrow on your return, please
     visit me

Rib Tickler

Why is our language called the mother tongue?

Because father never gets a chance to use it.

Autograph Verse

Jean Lunt from Mount Gambier, South Australia, sent in this entry from her school autograph album:

> Silently he stole to steal his bag of chinky chunk, many a silent smile he smole and many a wink he wunk.

TELEPHONE TIPS FROM THE TWENTIES

Nowadays we take telephones for granted and it's easy to forget that there was once a time when this method of communication was regarded with a degree of caution and even trepidation. However, it seems that the GPO were well-prepared for the nerves of the first-time users as they produced these helpful guidelines in 1923.

HOW TO PASS AND RECEIVE A TELEPHONE CALL

Passing a call

Before passing a call to the Exchange the subscriber should wait until he hears the telephonist's "Number, please?" and then, speaking CLEARLY and DISTINCTLY, with the lips **almost touching the mouthpiece**, he should state the number required.

FIRST the name of the Exchange and THEN the number. The method of pronouncing numbers in Telephone Exchanges has been devised to guard as far as possible against inaccuracies and a description of the system may be of assistance to subscribers.

It is important to remember that the distinctive sound of consonants become blurred in the transmission of speech by telephone and words containing the same vowels are apt to sound alike. Greater care is therefore necessary in speaking by telephone than is required in ordinary speech, if mistakes are to be avoided.

0 is pronounced as "OH", with long "O"			
1	"	"	**"WUN", emphasising the consonant "N"**
2	"	"	**"TOO", emphasising the consonant "T" and with long "OO"**
3	"	"	**"THR-R-EE", with slightly rolling "R" and long "E"**
4	"	"	**"FOER", one syllable with long "O"**
5	"	"	**"FIFE", emphasising the consonants "F"**
6	"	"	**"SIX", with long "X"**
7	"	"	**"SEV-EN", two syllables**
8	"	"	**"ATE", with long "A" and emphasising the consonant "T"**
9	"	"	**"NINE", one long syllable with long "I" and emphasising the consonants "N".**

Answering a call

The call should be answered promptly. On taking off the receiver, the called subscriber should not say "Hullo!" or "Who's there?" but should immediately announce his name.

A householder would say: "Mr. Thomas Brown speaking."

The maidservant: "Mr. Brown's house."

Mr. Brown, at his office, would say: "Brown & Co., Mr. Thomas Brown speaking."

His clerk: "Brown & Co."

Finish of conversation

The receiver should be replaced immediately the conversation is finished. Subscribers having Private Branch Exchange switchboards should ensure that adequate arrangements are made for PROMPT DISCONNECTION AT THE SWITCHBOARD. Neglect to do this may result in serious inconvenience.

A Nation of SHOPKEEPERS

The supermarket and the hypermarket reign supreme in this modern age of plastic decor, piped music and anonymous service. Or do they? From all corners of the land readers write to us every day to tell us of old-fashioned courtesy, personal attention and traditional values. Vast, neon-lit stores offering everything from bedroom suites to petrol may be taking over more and more, but there still exist across the nation small shopkeepers who cherish the long links with the communities of which they are an integral part. At *Evergreen* we think they deserve every encouragement, which is why we award a special diploma — a tribute to those who firmly believe in maintaining the character of their premises and the principles of personal, friendly service — which they can proudly display for all to see. Readers who would like to nominate their own favourite shop for our "Nation of Shopkeepers Award" should send brief details to the Editor.

There is one glory of Scotland that will never be found on a list of tourist attractions or in a visitor guide.

But to the people who travel from far and wide to patronise **James Pirie & Son** in the Angus village of Newtyle, the shop's championship winning sausages are just as much a source of Caledonian pride as Edinburgh Castle and Ben Nevis.

The family butcher's in the small rural community 12 miles from Dundee is not hard to find — but confirmation for visitors they have arrived at the right place is provided by a large sign boldly announcing: "Scottish Sausage Champions".

There is not enough room outside to reveal also that Pirie's saw off world-wide competition to capture gold and silver at an international food show in Holland, that it has taken the Scottish Meat Product of the Year title two years in a row — a unique achievement — and that among other supreme successes it has won the Tayside small business award for innovation.

But inside, plaques, medals and certificates and photographs of prizegiving ceremonies line every wall.

Among the trophies is a quartet — three golds and a bronze — won earlier this year at the Scottish Federation of Meat Traders' excellence event, when Pirie's entries were up against 180 other meat products.

That foursome brought the honours roll to 84, which is just one year less than the age of founder James Pirie — at 85 he is the oldest trading butcher in Scotland.

With son Alan at his side and Alan's wife Norma running the grocery and delicatessen next door he still does a full day, because his zest for work has never diminished since he launched the business more than 40 years ago.

"I wouldn't dream of slowing down", he says. "Dry rot would set in. I still enjoy meeting customers who have come from far and wide and I still enjoy my day-to-day work. It's what keeps me going."

What keeps his customers going, or rather coming, is a tantalising array of sausages, pies and pastries that have made James Pirie & Son famous throughout Scotland and beyond.

There are 36 varieties of sausage altogether, as well as haggis pies and speciality burgers, and Alan says some customers claim ("Tongue in cheek, I think") they can recite all 36 as easily as sing *Auld Lang Syne*.

It was an adventurous Scotch lamb, apple, mint and rosemary sausage that started it all off, and helped to drag the business from near disaster.

The Piries were renowned for

(continued overleaf)

(from previous page)

high-quality beef but during the BSE crisis in the Nineties struggled to survive as even loyal regulars scrapped the meat from their menu.

"We had to come up with some new ideas", says Alan, who joined his father five years after James founded the business in 1960, "otherwise we were facing a very bleak future.

"We had already been noted for our beef sausages, and when we began using lamb instead there was a favourable reaction.

"Then we came up with the brand new Scotch lamb, apple, mint and rosemary and our customers thought they were wonderful."

So did the judges for Scottish Meat Product of the Year. In 1996 they pronounced the innovative banger the best-tasting entrant by far.

The prizes and titles began rolling in. Three years later the Piries were named Scotland's Sausage Masters — this time for their traditional beef offerings that, with BSE fears ebbing, were making a welcome return.

The Pirie name spread. Alan says: "When we launched a new sausage, the Pride of Angus, people came in from miles around. One chap travelled from Aberdeen, 60 miles away, and went off with several kilos."

Like his father Alan believes that as well as a route to the customer's stomach you also need a route to the customer's heart.

"Personal service as well as good quality produce is essential", he says. "And it is important to make people feel welcome, whether they are regulars you know well or strangers."

Father and son also believe in rigorous sampling before launching a new recipe, with the chief tasters being Alan's two children, Gordon, 15, and Catrione, 17.

"They've not been wrong so far", Alan smiles. "If they like it, fine. If not, I go away and have another think.

"If products aren't good enough for the Pirie family they aren't good enough for the Pirie customers."

Mr. A. Denis Williams, of Dundee, who makes a round trip of 24 miles to shop at Pirie's, tells us: "The Piries are extremely well known for their adventurous sausages and on top of all that they and their excellent staff are forever obliging and friendly."

That is because, according to James, "the secret to still being able to work at 85 is a cheery disposition and a sincere interest in all the customers."

He pauses for thought: "Oh, and my Saturday night treat of sirloin steak."

There's another treat and another prize coming the way of you and your son, James — the Nation of Shopkeepers Award. We only hope you can find the space to display it!

DAVID FOSTER

Merville W. Gover has worked at **A.F. Joy**, of Wareham, since 1965. The shop is one of East Dorset's best-known menswear specialists, boasting fine country shirts; tweed jackets and blazers; a splendid line in dinner jackets, caps and striped night-shirts; a collection of trousers to suit any yeoman's waistline, plus, of course, excellent service and advice to match!

There is an atmosphere of the old England of the not-so-distant past, of discerning values, gentlemanly virtues and sheer quality.

Here Mr. Gover and his staff will go to any length to get you the right length. An alteration, something unusual, a particular make of jacket — nothing is too much trouble.

And the beauty of it is that A.F. Joy is part of a pleasant, traditional English High Street, mercifully free from the madness of overdevelopment and

Traditional service in a traditional shop: Merville W. Gover behind the counter he has helped to man for almost 40 years.

loud, vulgar shop-fronts.

Speaking to Mr. Gover is pleasant, too. "My Christian name is slightly unusual, isn't it?" he remarks.

"I am actually named after the town in Northern France where my father and his comrades were fighting for their lives in 1940 during the big retreat to the coast.

"His comrades died in action, and as a tribute to them he named me after this now sacred place."

He adds: "Living here is a privilege. Everything is still in its place, and I meet the same old friends in the pub each Friday evening. We still have rituals down here in Dorset!"

Congratulations to A.F. Joy — a true embodiment of everything held dear by this column.

STUART MILLSON

Up to now only a small percentage of the population will have been aware of the existence of the Anglo-Zulu War Historical Society, let alone its activities, but a new book brings it and its industrious gathering of new material to a far wider audience. **Redcoats and Zulus** (Pen & Sword, 224pp, hardback, £19.99), edited by Dr. Arian Greaves, is a collection of articles from the society's Journal and is from first to last unfailingly fascinating. In a tireless search for fresh insight and evidence the society has progressively uncovered previously unseen matter casting further light on a conflict that, going back though it does to 1879, still has ample capacity to engross. All the battles of the war are carefully considered from both sides with the best-known, Rorke's Drift — subject of the film *Zulu* — and Isandlwana coming under special scrutiny. Among the previously unseen diaries, personal accounts, correspondence, maps, diagrams and pictures the society has dug up are Lord Chelmsford's original orders following the slaughter at Isandlwana, one of the most calamitous defeats in British military history. They prove that the disaster was entirely Chelmsford's fault and not that of the brave officers who, killed in battle and unable to defend themselves, were made the scapegoats. Even now the injustice of it stirs to anger.

Cottages and farmhouses, barns and cow-houses, water mills and oast-houses — what do they all have in common? The third edition of Dr. R.W. Brunskill's **Traditional Buildings of Britain** (Cassell, 207pp, paperback, £25), informs us. In taking the story forward from the 19th to the late 20th century it carries further fine drawings from Dr. Brunskill's pen and a number of new photographs. But the most important addition is an extensive treatment of that mutual link — vernacular architecture. This, as the author lucidly explains, is the architecture of buildings that have in common the satisfaction of simple demands of family life, farming ways and industrial processes, are built out of materials to hand, and appear to belong to the district or region in which they are found. Many such sturdy structures, such as the Scottish crofter's cottage built with a minimum of skilled assistance but a maximum of passed-on experience, still exist and in their own robust way have as much attraction as lofty structures built of quarried stone and imported timber.

*   *   *

Between the two World Wars only the Americans showed any real cognisance of the potential of naval air power. Even the Imperial Japanese Navy had senior staff who felt it a kindness to discourage bright young officers from transferring from deck to cockpit. But during the Second World War the only major operations conducted without the benefit of carrier-borne aircraft were the Battle of the River Plate and the Anzio and Normandy landings. **Second World War Carrier Campaigns**, by David Wragg (Pen & Sword, 250pp, hardback, £19.99) describes the development of the huge flatships, as they came to be known, and of how effective they were in providing convoy protection and cover for invading ground forces. But, as might be expected, it is the story of the titanic battles fought between the huge carrier fleets of America and Japan as America fought its way across the Pacific that contains the most interest, and here it is arrestingly told. Ultimately, Japan came to regret embracing the carrier with the same enthusiasm as the United States. By launching its attack on Pearl Harbour from seaborne platforms that placed its aircraft within range, it sowed the seeds of its own destruction.

The 53 feet high Lundy North lighthouse, at the northern tip of Lundy Island in the Bristol Channel. See review this page.

*　　　*　　　*

It has never been satisfactorily explained why lighthouses are as alluring to landlubbers, who will travel as moths to a flame to see one, as they are an essential aid to mariners. Their fascination is further fed by Lynn F. Pearson in **Lighthouses** (Shire, 64pp, paperback, £4.99), which concentrates on the beacons, signal towers and other seamarks around our own shores but in a brief history also traces their history back to the fifth century BC, when the first were erected on the shores of the Mediterranean. She also reminds us that building beacons on rocks and reefs surrounded by heaving water was a challenge that required stoutness of heart as well as skill in engineering. This is a handy and interesting little volume for lighthouse lovers, especially as it has a selective gazetteer giving details of more than 160 of them.

*　　　*　　　*

When Iain Aitch decided to spend the summer travelling around England in search of the natives at leisure he found more eccentricity and drollness than he could possibly have hoped for, including, in a traditional Derbyshire pub, a toe-

More 'Bookshelf' overleaf

(continued)

wrestling competition where one contender was clad only in beer towels. Cornish villagers who float a giant pasty across a river each year, shin-kickers and crop-circle makers and Blackpool hen-parties all come under his diverting scrutiny in **A Fete Worse than Death** (Review, 304pp, paperback, £7.99). Even warm beer, wet weekends, the vagaries of the rail system and, occasionally, "a creeping feeling that the locals may not actually be a hundred per cent human", fail to spoil his fun.

*　　　*　　　*

For a restless young man wanting to escape the greyness of post-war Britain there was only one obvious thing to do — move to Kenya and fight the Mau-Mau. Alastair Tomkins, as he recounts in **A Beat Around the Bush** (Woodfield, 292pp, paperback, £9.95), never came to regret his decision, though his 10 years as a policeman combating the native terrorists attacking European farmers provided some perilous moments. The balance to the savagery that made headline news around the world was the dramatic scenery and exotic — and dangerous — wildlife, and the friends he made at every level of society in the former East African colony.

*　　　*　　　*

Odes, epics, sonnets, limericks, high verse and low doggerel — all have their place in **A Breathless Hush**, an MCC anthology of cricket verse. Edited by David Rayvern Allen with Hubert Doggart, the former Test player, it even contains Sir Tim Rice's libretto for the musical *Cricket*, which was commissioned by Prince Edward to mark the Queen's 60th birthday in 1986. But for capturing the drama of the game there is nothing here to match the verse by Sir Henry Newbolt from which the title is taken: "There's a breathless hush in the Close tonight — Ten to make and the match to win — A bumping pitch and a blinding light, An hour to play and the last man in". (Methuen, 492pp, hardback, £20).

*　　　*　　　*

The remarkable career of one of Britain's foremost architects is traced by Richard Tames in **Robert Adam** (Shire, 48pp, paperback, £4.99). In a concise but inclusive illustrated life, Richard Tames briskly surveys the career of an artist and architect whose name is as equated today with taste, style and elegance as it was by his contemporaries in the 18th century. So much so, in fact, that the term Adamesque has been randomly used to describe not only ceilings, doorways and fireplaces but a chamber-pot. Blessed with a rare vision that made him as gifted in decorating interiors as he was in the design of exteriors, a talented painter and deeply knowledgeable about classical architecture, the great Scot achieved something as rare in his day as his extraordinary talent — he became lionised by Society, achieved the dual status of artist and gentleman, and on his death in 1792 was deemed fit to be buried with kings at Westminster Abbey.

*　　　*　　　*

The full and fully-true story of the fall of Singapore still has to be told, and possibly never will be. From the day it was overrun, on 15th February 1942, an official curtain came down on information to conceal — though this was not admitted — the shame of craven surrender that cost the lives of many thousands of women and children as well as fighting men. It was not until Japanese prisoners-of-war began returning

in 1945 that eyewitness accounts started to emerge in any number, and even those, disparate and fragmentary, could not provide a complete picture. **Singapore's Dunkirk: the Aftermath of the Fall**, by Geoffrey Brooke (Pen & Sword, 256pp, hardback, £19.95) both shocks and inspires. Of 44 unescorted ships that managed to sail, mostly on the 13th, only one or two got through, and of the 5,000 mainly civilian people who fled just before and just after the disaster, a mere one in four avoided death or capture. The author himself was one of the few to escape and so he is well placed to talk of the great courage, extraordinary endurance and appalling atrocity and privation that marked those darkest of days.

*   *   *

Tom Sayers was a rugged London publican who had just become undisputed boxing champion of Britain, John Heenan a debonair American who had recently won his first professional fight. In times when bare-knuckle pugilism was a sport that

Elegant vista — Robert Adam's long gallery at Syon House, in Middlesex. See review opposite page.

drew followers from all levels of society both were hugely popular, and when they met in a Hampshire field to battle for the first world boxing championship in 1860 the event was a sporting sensation. The encounter, as grippingly recounted by Alan Lloyd in **The Great Prize Fight** (Souvenir Press, 188pp, paperback, £10.99) lasted 42 rounds and over two hours before it was stopped by the referee amid scenes of bedlam involving police and spectators, with neither of the hideously battered men declared the winner. Afterwards each was presented with a replica belt and Lord Palmerston, then Prime Minister, contributed to a fund set up for Sayers by his friends. The two fighters made a great deal of money from exhibitions and what would now be called celebrity appearances in the immediate aftermath, but both died destitute.

HENRY HARDCASTLE

Notices

EVERGREEN invites entries in these columns but reserves the right to refuse any advertisement. *Wordage rate:* £1 per word (minimum of 15 words). *Semi-display rate:* (House-style, no illustrations) £70.50 per single column inch. *Full-display rate:* £88.12 per single column inch (minimum size). All prices are inclusive of VAT and *must* be pre-paid. Current rate card sent on request. Send to: Evergreen Advertisements, PO Box 52, Cheltenham, Glos. GL50 1YQ, England, (Tel: 01242-537900) or E-mail: advert@thisengland.co.uk, no later than February 10th for inclusion in the Spring 2005 edition. Estimated current circulation: 48,000 copies.

Holidays/Accommodation

Devon Paignton Warm, friendly Apartments. Accommodates 1-2 persons in spacious comfort. Highly recommended. CH. Secluded beautifully landscaped gardens. Sun terrace. On-site Parking. Peaceful town centre Conservation area. Level stroll across park to excellent amenities and sandy beach, with breathtaking views across Torbay. Ideal location for exploring the delights of Devon. Non-smoking. No children. No pets. ETC****. Brochure with pleasure. Tel: 01803 558430.
www.alpenrose.myby.co.uk

London: B&B Centrally located comfortable family homes. Double £48, Single £34, Children's Reductions. Tel: 020 7385 4904.
www.thewaytostay.co.uk

Harbourside cottage — Porthleven, South Cornwall. Available all year. Well equipped. Warm welcome.Tel/Fax: 01326-565034 or
Tel: 01752 661351.

N. Yorks., Sowerby, Thirsk. Ideal touring dales and moors. Delightful flatlet, sleeps two, everything provided. No meters. Sorry no pets. Tel: 01845-522623.

Lincolnshire Farmhouse B&B, between coast and wolds. Idyllic retreat all year. Ensuite rooms £19pppn, disabled accessible. Ring for brochure. 01754 830316. www.willowfarmholidays.fsnet.co.uk

North Norfolk — Northrepps. Flint cottage, sleeps 2. Tastefully furnished. Garden. Parking. 2½ miles Cromer. Tel: 0208 755 4852.

Relaxing Canal Holidays on Britain's beautiful waterways. Comfortable self-drive boats. Middlewich Narrowboats. Tel: 44 (0) 1606-832460. Web: www.middlewichboats.co.uk. Fax: 44 (0) 1606-737912.

Fuengirola. Beautiful apartments, sleep 1-6. Car not essential. Walking distance to beach, bus, train. Tel: 0115 9320337. www.pueblalucia.com

Wilton, Salisbury. Comfortable well equipped flat. Sleeps three. £100-£115pw. Excellent holiday area. 01722-742127.

Devon/Somerset borders, family farm amidst peaceful, scenic countryside. Ideally situated Exmoor/Quantocks, coasts. Renowned for friendliness, comfort/delicious food. Ensuite available. ETB ♦♦♦♦. B&B £24 & Dinner £10, or BB&EM £34. Tel: Ann Heard 01398 361 296.

Wanted

Collector buys all fishing related items. — Anywhere in the UK. Reels, rods, flies, lures, stuffed fish, books, paintings, etc.
Phone: 07813-908999 anytime.

Always wanted — car and motoring programmes, brochures, catalogues, photos, magazines. Any amount. Tel: 01702-552624.

Wanted — Clocks and watches. Prefer broken, 01933 624296.

Aviation: Photographs and memorabilia by private collector. J. Gillingham, Harefield House, Main Road, Nutbourne, Chichester, PO18 8RS Tel: 01243 572272.

Old Provincial Theatre and Cinema programmes pre-1960 wanted by keen collector. G. Smith 39 Joydon Drive, Chadwell Heath, Essex RM6 4ST. 020 8597 4319.

Always Wanted: Collections of old 78 r.p.m. gramophone records: Opera, Ballads, Instrumental, Dance Bands, Jazz, Music Hall, Speech, etc. Mike Comber, 8 Inglewood Close, Warton, Nr. Preston, Lancashire PR4 1DX. Tel: 01772 679068.

Boy Scout Badges etc. wanted by collector. Graham Brooks, 28 Rawlin Close, Plymouth PL6 5TF. Tel: 01752-774467.

Collector/Carpenter — Woodworking hand tools. Tel: 01780-751768. B. Jackson, 10 Ayr Close, Stamford, Lincs. PE9 2TS.

Crafts & Gifts

Your music. Professional manuscripts from hand-written compositions. Singles, choir sets, extracts. Music Transcription Services, 45 Birmingham Road, Shenstone. WS14 0JS. +44(0)1543 480033.
Email: share@shenstone-staffs.fsnet.co.uk.

Birthday due? Give someone an original newspaper dated the very day they were born. £19 + free 1860's Times! 01492-531195.

CINE FILM TRANSFER
Your old 8mm or Super 8mm films *transferred to DVD or VHS video tape*
Further family or non commercial copies to DVD or VHS video tape
£5.00 only! (plus p&p, disk or tape)
Watch your memories instantly and without fuss on your TV screen. Add your old reel to reel or cassette recording or any backing of your choice. I can also edit, cut out, or add from other reels.
Talk to me, Ken, in the first instance!
01255 554939

Collecting

Magic lanterns, lantern slides, and related items sought by genuine collectors. Please phone 01825 830319.

Beermats, British Brewery and Cider sought by keen collector. Telephone Gerald, 01452 611498.

Postcards pre-1950 small or large collections required by a keen collector. Jenkins, 4 Chestnut Avenue, Christchurch, Dorset BH23 2PW.

Printed in England by St. Ives Direct, Hunters Armley, Bradford,
and published by This England Ltd., PO Box 52, Cheltenham, Glos., GL50 1YQ, U.K.

Back Issues

China Matching

Gardening

Books/Literary

Health

FOR A GOLF LOVER

Anyone who likes golf will love **The Man Who Inherited a Golf Course**. This super novel tells the story of Trevor Dukinfield who wakes up one morning to find that he is the owner of his very own golf club – fairways, bunkers, clubhouse and all. But to keep the club he must win a golf match, and he's never played a round of golf in his life. *"The scenario is tailor made for Vernon Coleman's light and amusing anecdotes about country life and pursuits"* said the Sunday Independent. *"Very readable!"* said Golf World. *"Hugely enjoyable in the best tradition of British comic writing"* said the Evening Chronicle. *"The mix of anecdotes and moments of sheer farce make for an absorbing read"* said the Evening Telegraph. A terrific present for anyone who enjoys golf– and more fun than another pair of socks! £12.95 hardback – over 19,000 copies sold.

... A CAT LOVER

Alice's Diary tells, with great humour and insight, of a year in the life of a mixed tabby cat. Our files are bursting with letters from readers who love this book. *"How wonderful ... so beautifully written, it was a pleasure to read"* wrote Mrs Y of Essex. *"Please send copies of Alice's Diary to the eleven friends on the accompanying list. It is a wonderful book which will give them all great pleasure,"* wrote Mr R of Lancashire. **Alice's Diary** is delightfully illustrated. A must for all animal lovers. £9.95 hardback – over 41,000 copies sold.

... A CRICKET LOVER

The Village Cricket Tour is a novel which describes the adventures and mishaps of a team of amateur cricketers who spend two weeks on a cricket tour of the West Country and which has been compared to Jerome K Jerome's classic "Three Men in a Boat". *"I enjoyed it immensely"* wrote Peter Tinniswood in Punch. *"He has succeeded in writing a book that will entertain, a book that will amuse and warm the cockles of tired hearts."* *"Coleman is a very funny writer,"* said This England. *"All the characters are here, woven together by a raft of anecdotes and reminiscences and a travelogue of some of the most picturesque spots in the South West."* A great gift for cricket lovers. £12.95 hardback – over 25,000 copies sold.

The Perfect Present

Solve your present buying problems NOW by choosing from this selection of beautifully bound and jacketed hardback books from best-selling author

Vernon Coleman

"Vernon Coleman writes brilliant books" THE GOOD BOOK GUIDE

OUR GUARANTEE
If, for any reason, you are not happy with your books then simply return them to us in good condition within 28 days and we will refund the purchase price.

To order by post send details of the books you would like, your name, address and your cheque/PO (payable to Publishing House) to: Publishing House (EV15), Trinity Place, Barnstaple, Devon EX32 9HJ, England. *Please add £1 per book towards p&p in the UK.* **To order using your credit card** please call our 24 hour Orderline on 01271 328892 and quote **EV15** (your call will be answered by a real person!). We look forward to hearing from you.

Evergreen Melodies

Presenting yesterday's music for your listening pleasure today!

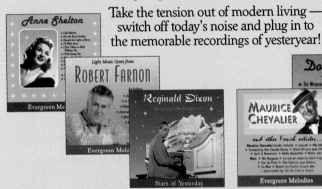

Take the tension out of modern living — switch off today's noise and plug in to the memorable recordings of yesteryear!

◄ NEW RELEASE

Our tapes and CDs continue to grow in number and popularity. Even the youngsters enjoy listening to them! You can't buy them in any record shop — they are only available direct from *Evergreen*.

CD PRICE only £8.95 each (inc. UK post)
Overseas surface mail (airmail in brackets)
£10 (£11); or US $18 (20); Can $24 (27); Aus $27 (30); NZ $31 (34).

CD
£8.95
inc. UK post

TAPE
£7.50
inc. UK post

Tape PRICE only £7.50 (inc. UK post)
Overseas surface mail (airmail in brackets)
£8.50 (£9.50) or US $15 (17); Can $21 (23); Aus $23 (26); NZ $26 (29).

Special Offer: Buy any 3 tapes — choose a fourth one FREE!
N.B. This offer does not apply to CDs

Tapes play for approx. 45 minutes, but most CDs have extra tracks.

Evergreen, PO Box 52, Cheltenham, Glos. GL50 1YQ.
Telephone sales: 01242-515156 (all major cards accepted)

	Tape	CD
Robert Farnon	●	●
English Hymns	●	●
Reginald Dixon	●	●
Boy Sopranos	●	●
Noel Coward	●	●
Ivor Novello	●	●
Laurel & Hardy	●	●
Josef Locke	●	●
Albert Ketèlbey	●	●
Carroll Gibbons	●	●
The Ink Spots	●	●
Anne Shelton	●	●
Al Bowlly	●	●
Perry Como	●	●
Paul Robeson	●	●
Frank Sinatra	●	●
Danny Kaye	●	●
Jessie Matthews	●	●
Hubert Gregg	●	●
Sam Costa	●	●
'Hutch'	●	●
Albert Sandler	●	●
Henry Hall	●	●
Elsie Carlisle	●	●
Peter Dawson	●	●
Evelyn Laye	●	●
Donald Peers	●	●
Fred Astaire	●	●
Kate Smith	●	●
Rarities 1	●	●
Rarities 2		●
Patience Strong	●	●
Richard Tauber	●	●
Joyce Grenfell	●	●
Semprini	●	●
Monte Rey	●	●
Richard Crooks	●	●
Vera Lynn	●	●
Eric Coates	●	●
George Formby	●	●
George Elrick	●	●
Frank Crumit	●	●
Arthur Tracy	●	●
Steve Conway	●	●
Monologues	●	●
Denny Dennis	●	●
Spike Jones	●	●
Nat Temple	●	●
Stephen Foster	●	●

	Tape	CD
Our Gracious Queen	●	●
The Ovaltineys	●	●
Life with the Lyons	●	●
Stanley Holloway 1	●	●
Stanley Holloway 2	●	
Kenneth Alford	●	●
The Voice of Churchill	●	●
Dance Band Signatures	●	●
Dance Band Rarities		●
Dance Band Vocalists		●
Stephane Grappelli	●	●
Kathleen Ferrier	●	●
Christmas Celebration	●	●
John McCormack	●	●
Flanagan & Allen	●	●
Rawicz & Landauer	●	●
George Shearing	●	●
Cavan O'Connor	●	●
Chick Henderson	●	●
Bob & Alf Pearson	●	
Children's Favourites	●	●
Layton & Johnstone	●	●
Harry Davidson	●	●
Kentucky Minstrels	●	●
Dorothy Lamour	●	
The Mills Brothers	●	●
B. Hale & B. Howes	●	●
Father MacEwan	●	●
Playing the Halls	●	●
Evergreen Country	●	●
Cowboy Songs	●	●
Music Hall Memories	●	●
J. Shand & R. Wilson	●	●
Radio/TV Themes 1	●	●
Radio/TV Themes 2	●	●
Radio/TV Themes 3	●	●
Parlour Poetry	●	●
Jack Buchanan	●	●
Sandy Macpherson	●	●
Songs of Britain	●	●
Sing a Song of England	●	●
Black & White Minstrels	●	●
Five Smith Brothers	●	●
A. Ziegler & W. Booth	●	●
N. Eddy & J. MacDonald	●	●
I. Moreton & D. Kaye	●	●
Vaughan Monroe	●	●
Alfred Piccaver	●	●
Max Bygraves	●	●

TAPES ●   CDs ●

	Tape	CD
Bob Hope	●	
Tom Burke	●	●
Double Acts		●
Louis Levy	●	●
Peter Yorke	●	
Sisters	●	
Maurice Chevalier	●	●
Luton Girls Choir	●	●
Railway Music	●	
Our Finest Hour	●	●
Spirit of Victory	●	●
Lest We Forget	●	●
Charlie Kunz 1 & 2	●	●
Search for a Song 1, 2 & 3	●	
Deanna Durbin 1 & 2	●	
Deanna Durbin*		●
Concert Ballads 1	●	
Concert Ballads*		●
Gracie's Comic Songs	●	
Gracie Fields 1, 2 & 3	●	
Gracie Fields*		●
Bing Crosby 1, 2 & 3	●	
Bing Crosby*		●

CD — selection from the tapes

A Year to Remember

	CD
1926/27/28/29	●
1930/31/32/33/34	●
35/36/37/38/39	●
1940/41/42/43/44	●

(see page 117)

Songs from the Shows
Songs & tunes from London musicals.

	Tape	CD
Edwardian Shows	●	●
G & S Overtures	●	●
G & S Songs	●	●
1st World War	●	●
The Twenties	●	●
The Thirties	●	●
Vivian Ellis	●	●
2nd World War	●	●
Harry Parr Davies	●	●
The Roaring Forties	●	●
Billy Mayerl	●	●
American Fifties	●	●
Noel Coward	●	●
Show-Stoppers	●	●
The British Fifties	●	●

ORDER FORM & CATALOGUE DETAILS OVERLEAF

SEND FOR OUR FREE MUSIC CATALOGUE

This updated version contains complete track listings of all our CDs, tapes and albums.

Such a varied selection of ballads, dance band music, rare and unusual sounds from the past, music hall, songs from shows, historic speeches and much more, gives a wide choice to suit all tastes.

☐ *Tick box for the music catalogue*

To save time you can order by telephone on 01242-515156

			FOR OFFICE USE ONLY
Name/Address: _____			
_____			
_____ Postcode: _____			
Your Telephone Number:			
▼ Fill in titles & tick coloured boxes for tape or CD	TAPE	CD	
I enclose payment of_____ by cheque/credit card			
Card no: ☐☐☐☐☐☐☐☐☐☐☐☐☐☐☐☐			
Expiry Date: Signature:	Switch Issue no: ☐☐		

ALL MAJOR CREDIT CARDS ACCEPTED

If you do not want to cut the page, send details on a separate piece of paper.

Evergreen, PO Box 52, Cheltenham, Gloucestershire, GL50 1YQ.

BACK NUMBERS

If you have missed previous editions of *Evergreen*, a small supply of the back numbers listed below are still available. Remember you can order *Evergreen* subscriptions, books, binders, and back numbers, etc. over the telephone on **(01242) 515156** (all major cards accepted). Since we prefer to handle your calls personally, please telephone us during normal office hours: 9 am to 5.30 pm Monday to Friday. If you would rather order back numbers by post, please fill in the form below and send it, with your remittance, to the address at the bottom of the page. Brief details about the contents of each back issue are included in a free leaflet, available from *Evergreen*.

Choose from the following list — tick boxes of issues required

1985	1987	1988	1989	1990
☐ SUMMER	☐ SPRING	☐ SPRING	☐ SPRING	☐ SPRING
☐ AUTUMN	☐ SUMMER	☐ SUMMER	☐ SUMMER	☐ SUMMER
☐ WINTER	☐ AUTUMN	☐ AUTUMN	☐ AUTUMN	☐ AUTUMN
	☐ WINTER		☐ WINTER	☐ WINTER

1991	1992	1993	1994	1995
☐ SPRING	☐ SPRING	☐ SPRING	☐ SPRING	☐ SPRING
☐ SUMMER	☐ SUMMER	☐ SUMMER	☐ SUMMER	☐ SUMMER
☐ AUTUMN	☐ AUTUMN	☐ AUTUMN	☐ AUTUMN	☐ AUTUMN
☐ WINTER	☐ WINTER	☐ WINTER	☐ WINTER	☐ WINTER

1996	1997	1998	1999	2000
☐ SPRING	☐ SPRING	☐ SPRING	☐ SPRING	☐ SPRING
☐ WINTER	☐ SUMMER	☐ SUMMER	☐ SUMMER	☐ SUMMER
	☐ AUTUMN	☐ AUTUMN	☐ AUTUMN	☐ AUTUMN
		☐ WINTER	☐ WINTER	☐ WINTER

2001	2002	2003	2004	
☐ SPRING	☐ SPRING	☐ SPRING	☐ SPRING	
☐ SUMMER	☐ SUMMER	☐ SUMMER	☐ SUMMER	
☐ AUTUMN	☐ AUTUMN		☐ AUTUMN	
☐ WINTER				

PRICES: including postage and packing:

One copy to UK **£3.75** (£4.50 overseas) US $8; Can $11; Aus $12; NZ $14.
4 copies to UK **£9** (£10.50 overseas) US $19; Can $26; Aus $28; NZ $32.
10 copies to UK **£20** (£23 overseas) US $41; Can $56; Aus $62; NZ $71.

NAME/ADDRESS: _____

_____

_____ POSTCODE: _____

If you don't want to cut this page send details in on a separate sheet

---

When completed, post with remittance, to: Evergreen, PO Box 52, Cheltenham, Glos. GL50 1YQ.

The gift of Evergreen ...

Enjoy the old-fashioned pleasure of giving a simple gift to your friends and relatives at home and abroad by sending them a subscription to *Evergreen*. As each edition arrives through the year they will be reminded of your kind thought.

Subscription Rates: *4 editions inc. postage and packing*
To UK addresses £15.00   To Overseas addresses £17.50

Payment from abroad (if not paying in sterling)
USA $32   Canada $43   Australia $48   New Zealand $56

If ordering by post, please print your name and address in the Donor panel below.
Use other panels when ordering gift subscriptions for friends.

DONOR

FOR OFFICE USE ONLY

When acknowledging your order for gift subscriptions we send you an exclusive Greetings Card, with envelope, for you to sign and send on to your friends, announcing your gift.

NAME: _____

ADDRESS: _____

_____

_____

POSTCODE:

If taking out a subscription for **yourself** tick this box ☐   £/$

Is this a new subscription? ☐   Or a renewal? ☐

To start with the   edition

GIFT FORM 1

FOR OFFICE USE ONLY

NAME: _____

ADDRESS: _____

_____

_____

POSTCODE:

Please post Evergreen for one year to the above ☐   £/$

Is this a new subscription? ☐   Or a renewal? ☐

To start with the   edition

GIFT FORM 2

FOR OFFICE USE ONLY

* Subscriptions will commence with the **next** edition unless otherwise requested. Although we aim to deal with all orders on receipt, please allow up to 14 working days for postal delivery.

NAME: _____

ADDRESS: _____

_____

_____

POSTCODE:

Please post Evergreen for one year to the above ☐   £/$

Is this a new subscription? ☐   Or a renewal? ☐

To start with the   edition